TRUSTS FOR THE AVERAGE PERSON

THE OPTIMUM ESTATE PLAN

A practical guide to avoiding probate, nursing-home costs and estate taxes

Edward D. Beasley, JD, LLM

David H. Ferber, JD

Gregory B. Gagne, ChFC

Library of Congress Control No: 2008903351
ISBN-13: 978-0-9789845-1-9
ISBN-10: 0-9789845-1-X

Printed in the United States of America by Mennonite Press, Inc.
Newton, Kansas

Book Design by Sandi Nelsen

Published by Beasley & Ferber, PA, Concord, New Hampshire, and Affinity Investment Group, LLC, Exeter, New Hampshire.

For Additional copies, send $24.95 plus $3.00 shipping and handling per book to:

Beasley & Ferber, PA
55 Hall Street
Concord, NH 03301 (603) 225-5010
                    or
Affinity Investment Group, LLC
18 Hampton Road, Unit 7
Exeter, NH 03833
(603) 778-6436

Dedication

*T*his book is dedicated to the memory of my late father, Abraham Ferber, who had the foresight to have his legal affairs put in order when he was healthy enough to do so, thereby making my job infinitely easier at the time of his passing.

David Ferber

Table of Contents

About the Authors

*E*dward D. Beasley, JD, LLM, is the founder of Beasley & Ferber, P.A., an estate planning and elder law firm with offices in Concord, Bedford, and Nashua, New Hampshire and North Andover, Massachusetts. He received his Bachelor's Degree, Summa Cum Laude, Phi Beta Kappa from Dartmouth College (1974), his Juris Doctor Degree, Cum Laude, from Washington & Lee University (1978) and his LLM Degree in Taxation from Boston University (1982).

Mr. Beasley has written and published numerous articles on estate planning and elder law and has appeared as a panelist on many elder law and estate planning symposiums. He has appeared as a featured guest on NBC's Nightly News with Tom Brokaw in a segment entitled, "Inheritance Disputes." Attorney Beasley was also featured in a USA Today cover story entitled, "Fighting Over the Care of Aging Parents." He is co-author of the books, "Alzheimer's Disease: Fighting for Financial Survival," "The Nursing Home Crunch," "Asset Protection & Retirement in New Hampshire" and "Asset Protection & Retirement in Massachusetts."

Mr. Beasley is former Chair of the Elder Law Committee of the American Bar Association. He is also a member of the National Academy of Elder Law Attorneys. Mr. Beasley is recognized nationally as an expert in the fields of elder law, Medicaid, and nursing home planning and asset preservation techniques for those afflicted with mental, physical, and developmental disabilities. He is a recipient of Martindale-Hubbell's highest "AV" peer review rating.

Attorney Beasley is a member of the bars of New Hampshire, Massachusetts, Rhode Island, and Virginia.

*D*avid H. Ferber, JD, is a partner with Beasley & Ferber, P.A. He received his Bachelor's Degree in Psychology, Magna Cum Laude, Phi Beta Kappa from Columbia University (1981) and his Juris Doctor Degree from Columbia University Law School (1984) where he was a member of the Columbia Human Rights Law Review.

Mr. Ferber is a nationally published author of articles on estate and Medicaid planning, including articles on the Deficit Reduction Act, the joint revocable trust as a tool for estate and Medicaid planning, annuities in Medicaid Planning, among others. He is also the author of articles on estate planning for the Concord Monitor, Concord, N.H. and the Laconia Citizen, Laconia, N.H. He is co-author of the books, "Alzheimer's Disease: Fighting for Financial Survival," "The Nursing Home Crunch," "Asset Protection & Retirement in New Hampshire" and "Asset Protection & Retirement in Massachusetts." He is a frequent lecturer on estate and Medicaid planning, having given presentations on estate planning for other attorneys, social workers/case managers and the general public. He has been a guest on WMUR-TV and WGIR-Radio, speaking about nursing home planning.

Mr. Ferber is former Vice-Chair and Newsletter Editor of

the Elder Law Committee of the American Bar Association and is a member of the National Academy of Elder Law Attorneys. He is a member of the bars of New Hampshire, Massachusetts, Maine, and Connecticut.

*G*regory B. Gagne, ChFC, is the founder of Affinity Investment Group, LLC, an investment advisory firm registered with the United States Securities and Exchange Commission. His firm offers wealth management and distribution planning services for retirees or those planning to retire.

After earning his Bachelor of Science, a dual degree in economics and finance, from Bentley College in 1992, Mr. Gagne became a Chartered Financial Consultant in 2001 following completion of courses in estate planning, financial planning, business planning, income tax, and retirement and pension planning through the American College.

A member of the New Hampshire Chapter of the Society of Financial Service Professionals, Mr. Gagne is also past president of the New Hampshire Association of Insurance and Financial Advisors, having served previously in many chairs of its local board. He now serves on a national committee for the organization.

Mr. Gagne has garnered national exposure in professional trade magazine articles and is co-author of the book, "Asset Protection & Retirement in New Hampshire." He frequently is featured writing on topics such as practice management, planning techniques, and goal setting. He is a sought-after speaker on these subjects.

Introduction

*M*y career in the practice of law, and the start of my love for estate planning, began almost 30 years ago in January of 1979. I was practicing as an associate for a large law firm in Nashua, New Hampshire. I was assigned to the corporate department, as opposed to the litigation department, where the legal work varied from real estate to business to taxation and estate planning. Many lawyers, including those in our own firm, considered estate planning dull and boring— certainly not on the level of trial work and litigation. To me, estate planning, in its own way, was every bit as exciting as trial work; it was positive in the sense that we estate planners worked together with the client's team of professionals (financial planners, certified public accountants, and stockbrokers) to reach an optimum goal or plan for our clients.

For me, the excitement was in the realization that each client presented a set of facts—past experiences and future hopes—unique entirely to them. Each client needed a customized plan crafted to fit their individualized needs, which defied a "one-size-fits-all" solution. It was also during these early years that I became aware of the power of trusts in estate planning. Many folks today don't realize that trusts have been around for decades, albeit mostly for the affluent, and were commonly used in the law firm where I began my career. These trusts were designed primarily to avoid or eliminate estate taxation. During this time, I earned a master's degree in taxation from Boston University, which has proven invaluable to me. Knowledge of tax law plays an integral part in estate planning, even for average folks.

After several years, I accepted a position with another, small law firm as the head of its estate-planning department. This law firm specialized in construction law, representing mostly small, family-owned businesses. Unlike my first law firm, which tended to represent fairly wealthy folks, this law firm represented mostly average- to slightly above-average financial net-worth folks. My job was to facilitate the passage of these small, family businesses from one generation to the next. Many of the clients I represented were elderly parents looking to transfer ownership of their businesses to their children with minimum hassles, estate or gift taxation, and publicity. While many of these families were above-average in terms of financial net worth, most were not. However, each and every estate plan was as unique as the facts and circumstances of the lives of the people for whom it was prepared. Again, there was no one-size-fits-all plan, but virtually every estate plan we prepared incorporated some kind of trust as a vital component. In many cases, the trusts we created for our clients in this law firm were solely intended to avoid the hassles, legal fees, delays, and publicity of the probate process.

The final phase of my career began 20 years ago with the establishment of Beasley & Ferber, P.A. The goals of Attorney David Ferber and myself from the very start were to represent average folks and make available to them the exact same services and protections afforded wealthier clients of larger law firms. Our initial objectives for all our clients were two-fold: avoid probate, where appropriate, and avoid or eliminate estate taxation. In time, we added a crucial, third objective to our mission statement: avoid loss of everything to a prolonged stay in a nursing home. In many ways, this third objective was the most crucial in all our planning. What good did it do to devise and implement an otherwise "ideal" estate plan if, at the eleventh hour, the client or client's spouse entered a nursing home and the entire net worth was depleted for the spouse's care? We knew that many of our clients wanted to legally protect their lifetime savings both for themselves, their spouses, and ultimately, their children. We knew, from experience, that many of our clients simply wanted to save their home from "spend-down" to a nursing home stay. Most importantly, we knew that through the use of trusts and other sophisticated strategies, our clients' goals of nursing-home asset protection could be legally achieved.

We have been asked by some whether the nursing home component of our planning is ethical. Is it, in fact, ethical to devise an estate plan that legally protects some, if not all, assets from nursing-home costs and state-required spend-down? Our answer is, and has always been, that it's ethical to show our clients how to protect their assets, if that is what they want. After all, the rich client is advised by his attorney on how to avoid estate taxes through complicated, generation-skipping type trusts and other strategies, and no one seems to think they are doing something unethical. In fact, they are almost universally admired for realizing a need and addressing it. In our opinion, our average client who establishes a Medicaid Trust to protect his assets from nursing home spend-down is no different from the rich business owner who establishes a Creditor Protection Trust to insulate his assets from loss to creditors. Our experience shows that estate planning for average folks is, in one regard, the same as estate planning for rich folks: both want to legally preserve what they have for their spouse and family. After all, the rich client's mansion and millions invested in the stock market are no more important to him than the average client's house, IRA and Certificate of Deposit. Not only is it ethical to plan to protect assets for rich and average folks alike, it would be, in our opinion, unethical not to do so if asked.

As a result of over 50 years of combined practice in estate planning, the concept of an ideal, perfect, or "optimum" estate plan has become clear to us. Almost without exception, our clients wish to avoid the hassles, legal fees, costs, delays, and publicity of probate. This can easily be eliminated by the use of a traditional Revocable Trust, also known as a "living trust." Almost without exception, our clients wish to avoid or eliminate the payment of estate taxes. This can be accomplished for married couples by the use of two Revocable Trusts, one for each spouse, and by single folks through the technique of lifetime gifting. Almost without exception, our clients wish to avoid losing all their assets to a prolonged stay in the nursing home. This can be accomplished by the Irrevocable Medicaid Trust, in combination with other strategies we describe in this book. In addition, experience has shown us that most folks don't simply die suddenly in their sleep. Yes, this does happen, but it is generally preceded, as in the case of my own dad, by a period of failing physical and mental capacities. Almost without exception, our clients wish for an orderly transition of control of their financial and medical affairs in the event of their incapacity. Properly drafted Durable Financial and Health Care Powers of Attorney or Proxies can accomplish this goal. Our clients want to ensure that there are no loose ends, which can arise after death. This is accomplished through the use of a Pour-over Will.

We know from experience that an optimum plan must address all of the above, and that virtually every estate plan must have certain vital documents. These documents consist of the following:

1. Pour-over Wills
2. Revocable Trusts
3. Irrevocable "Medicaid" Trusts
4. Durable Powers of Attorney
5. Health Care Powers of Attorney and Living Wills

The Optimum Estate Plan for average folks uses all five of these documents at the same time. As you will see in the following chapters, the plan has two different trusts operating in conjunction: the Revocable Trust to avoid probate and estate taxation, where appropriate, and the Medicaid Trust to avoid probate and loss to a nursing home. The Pour-over Will provides a mechanism to catch something accidentally not placed into one trust or the other. The Durable Powers of Attorney for Finance and Health Care and the Living Will may be the most crucial documents of all to provide proper transition in the event of physical or mental disability.

Finally, the Optimum Estate Plan for average folks must maximize our clients' financial planning. After all, of what good is a plan to pass assets among spouses and children if our clients outlive their money? Maximizing financial return in retirement, be it to minimize income taxes to be paid or maximize income generated, is a key financial goal. Noted financial planner, Gregory Gagne, has offered valuable insights in this book on these financial matters. Most clients share a common primary objective of protecting the assets they have spent a lifetime building, especially protecting their spouse if married. The second major objective for clients is insuring a legacy can be passed to their children and hopefully grandchildren if planned appropriately. Unfortunately, many seniors have done a lackluster job preparing for the proper protection and transition of their assets. People don't plan to fail... they fail to plan. We will spend time in this book exploring many of the major obstacles to protecting assets. Numerous legal planning options will be addressed. Trusts, when used properly, will help you safeguard your non-retirement related assets. Retirement accounts, however, (we will refer to these as IRAs going forward) cannot be held in trust and thus must be dealt with utilizing other planning strategies. For many retirees other than the primary residence, the IRA account is one of the largest assets on the personal net worth statement. The combination of income tax, estate tax, and nursing home spend-down can devastate these accounts. This should not occur, and with well thought-out planning executed in advance, it won't.

Our goal for you as you read this book is to dovetail our unique approach of estate planning legal techniques in conjunction with prudent financial planning to create for you and your family the OPTIMUM ESTATE plan.

Ted Beasley

Chapter 1
The Genesis of the Optimum Estate Plan

*W*e have been practicing estate planning for decades. During that time, we have helped thousands of families in New Hampshire and Massachusetts avoid probate, estate taxes, and protect their homes and lifetime savings from prolonged nursing-home stays. In general, we've also helped plan for sheltering assets and passing them to our clients' children. Our first priority is, and always has been, to make sure surviving spouses are afforded the best quality of life financially available to them after their spouse's death. Next, we work to ensure that what we perceive as onerous Medicaid spend-down rules do not impoverish a healthy spouse when his or her spouse is confined to a nursing home. After all, this is traumatic and emotionally devastating enough. Our second priority is to ensure that our client's lifetime savings are passed down to his children with as little loss from probate, taxes, or nursing-home care as possible.

Often, our work is routine: meeting with average, retired people in our office or the comfort of their home at a leisurely pace to make sure the estate plan is done just right. It must work efficiently upon the death of our client, but it also must work as a life plan in the event our client becomes physically or mentally disabled. Sometimes, the work is urgent: both of us have rushed to hospitals, nursing homes, or hospice houses to meet with people who have not done advanced planning, and who have days or even hours to live. Other times, we work with the adult children of nursing-home patients to make sure that Medicaid is approved, or to help protect the parents' home or lifetime savings from being consumed by the nursing home. Or, we go to Probate court to settle an estate, or apply for guardianship over someone with Alzheimer's Disease or dementia. The work is challenging, often frustrating, sometimes routine, but never, ever dull.

Nothing, however, makes us understand our clients and their needs more than being in their shoes, living in their angst. My parents, Doug and Betty, retired to Cape Cod in 1978. They were of modest means, my mom's folks having been wiped out in the Depression and my dad having suffered through a corporate bankruptcy just before retiring. They had a home and very modest financial assets. In the early 1980s, I did a rather basic estate plan for them, consisting of a Revocable Trust to avoid probate, plus wills, and Financial and Health Care Durable Powers of Attorney (Proxies). At that time, nursing-home planning was not part of my parents' estate plan, inasmuch as the cost of long-term care in nursing homes was not prohibitive and the laws in place then allowed for more flexibility in last-minute planning. My dad outlived my mom, and the plan I'd prepared for the two of them worked perfectly. It allowed him to care for my mom during the year she battled with cancer, and then continue on without the hassles of probate after she died. Then, I updated my dad's plan, which included revisions to his existing Revocable Trust, Durable Power of Attorney and Health Care Proxy.

I also sat down with my dad and two brothers, Doug and Ray, after my mom died, to vigorously discuss the topic of dad's future, potential nursing-home care, and resulting loss of life savings. After all, my dad was still a vibrant, "young," 68-year-old widower and a potential nursing-home stay seemed unlikely, or at least many years away. However, my dad—having lived through the Depression and having lost almost everything due to bankruptcy—wanted to ensure that, at a minimum, his house would be protected for my brothers and me. I prepared an Irrevocable Medicaid Trust for my dad expressly to protect his house from a possible, future nursing-home stay. At first, my dad balked at the concept of doing anything "irrevocable." I remember him saying, to paraphrase, "I don't want to be put in a box." I walked him through the details of the trust, how it worked and precisely how, as a trustee, my dad was not losing control; he wasn't being "put in a box." I assured my dad that he could sell his house, move to Florida, and buy another, if he wanted, and that he could even disinherit one or more of his sons. In summary, the Medicaid Trust, while irrevocable, gave my dad the kind of flexibility he wanted at his still-young age. My dad's limited financial assets remained in the Revocable Trust, totally accessible to him at all times.

Once the plan was revised and implemented, my dad and brothers essentially forgot it was in place. This all changed about 12 years later when my dad began showing increased signs of forgetfulness. Gradually, his overall health declined, and he went from having an active lifestyle to being shut in at home. He developed dementia, and was cared for at home by my brothers. I remember vividly a discussion with my brothers about the possibility that they might not be able to care for dad because of his increased health issues, and that a nursing home might be inevitable. While this was emotional for all of us, I remember that my dad, even in his limited capacity, took great comfort in the knowledge that no matter what happened to him, at least his house—his one major asset—was protected for us. Eventually, dad died in his sleep, at home. Due to the work I'd done, there was no probate or other legal hassles in transferring my dad's assets to us. To this day, I'm grateful that the plan I prepared, well in advance, gave my dad comfort and peace of mind in his final years.

In December 2006, David's father, Abraham, a widower who lived in Florida, was diagnosed with melanoma. He went through surgery, radiation, and chemotherapy, but nothing worked. By July 2007, his dad's condition had deteriorated noticeably. By October of that year, he had gotten so weak and debilitated that it was not safe for him to live at home. Arrangements were made for him to go to a nursing home. The placement was made on a Thursday, and he was supposed to be admitted the following Monday. On that Friday, however, he died.

David writes about the work he did for his father and the experience with such work:

"Ten years ago, after my father retired and while he was still in perfect health, he asked me to put together an estate plan for him. I did, and it included the same documents that Ted had prepared for his father. Little did I know that I would experience, first hand, the power of these documents. Prior to my trip to Florida to see my father, I called his oncologist to find out about my father's condition. The doctor, though, was not able to talk to me due to federal medical privacy rules. Once I sent the doctor a copy of the Medical Power of Attorney, containing a "HIPAA medical authorization," however, the doors opened: the doctor could talk to me. I made the trip to Florida. What I found amazed and shocked me. My father has always had the benefit of "good genes." Until almost the end, he had a full head of black hair and was as robust as someone 20 years his junior. However, the illness had devastated him.

He was bedridden and could barely move. Knowing that he had no ability to pay his bills anymore, I took my father's Durable Power of Attorney, naming me as agent, to the bank. The bank officer was able to use this document to give me signing authority over his bank accounts. Thus, I was able to start paying his bills and managing his finances for him without any problem. After he died, his two trusts sprang into action. His house was in the Irrevocable Medicaid Trust. Since a trust avoids probate, I was able to have the deed transferred into my name quickly and easily. The same held true for the assets in his Revocable Trust. His modest estate was completely settled within two months of his death (it actually could have been done faster, but I was not in a hurry) without any hassles, at a trivial cost, and with no legal fees—not because I was a lawyer, but because my father had the trusts in place.

All of my father's documents served their own special purpose. They all worked flawlessly and seamlessly to assure a quick, smooth, and efficient transition of the assets from him to me. In the space of a year, from his diagnosis to his death, I had gone through what many of our clients have gone through, and the experience of being "on the other side of the desk," so to speak, has enabled me to speak to our clients from a different perspective. While nothing, even well-done legal documents, could have alleviated my emotional angst at the death of my father, the legal work allowed me, from afar in New Hampshire, to settle his affairs in short time and with minimum energy. I could move on with my life, which, after all, was my father's hope."

Out of these experiences with clients and our own fathers was born the concept of the Optimum Estate Plan. Of course, everyone is different, and what works for one client might not work for another. However, the issues and documents we discuss in the following pages, or some variation of them, will apply to all of our readers. This is not intended to be a lengthy, complex, legal tome, but a straightforward, average person's guide to protecting assets from probate fees and expenses, estate taxes, and nursing-home costs.

Chapter 2
Wills And Revocable Trusts

A. The Last Will and Testament

Your last will and testament is, of course, a legal document that states where your assets are to go when you die. A surprising number of people think that what you say in your will happens automatically, or that the person you name as executor simply implements what the will says, and that the courts and legal system do not get involved. However, generally the opposite is true. Except between spouses, where most of their assets—if not all—are owned in joint names and pass outside the will automatically by law to the surviving spouse, a will is generally going to be subject to Probate court proceedings. A will, it has been said, is your family's admission ticket to probate. What exactly is probate, and, when someone dies, what happens to his or her will?

To demonstrate why trusts, not wills, are the most important documents in transferring assets upon death, it is useful to trace the path that a will takes upon the death of an individual. When you die, your will is filed with the Probate court for the county where you lived, along with a petition for appointment of an executor. It is not the case that the person you name as executor automatically becomes so on your death. When you name someone in your will to act as executor, it is a nomination. Only the Probate court has legal authority to appoint an executor. The court will almost always follow your suggestion, but it is not required to do so.

For example, say you nominate your son as executor. Some years after you have signed your will, your son is convicted of embezzlement, or tax evasion, or fraud, and goes to jail. You fail to change your will and pass away with your son still named as executor. Since being an executor is a position of trust and confidence, and requires him to handle money, it is unlikely that the court will honor your will and appoint him as executor. Or, less dramatically, your son may die before you or become disabled and, therefore, be unable to serve as executor. In this case, the court has no choice but to appoint someone else to perform the duties of wrapping up your estate.

Another common fallacy is that there is a "reading of the will" by the decedent's attorney. While this can make for a dramatic scene in a murder mystery, in real life, the will is generally not read at a meeting of the family shortly after someone dies. As mentioned above, the will is filed with the local Probate court, where it becomes a public document. Anyone may obtain a copy and read it.

What constitutes a valid will? Even if a document has the word "will" in the title, it does not automatically qualify as one under state law. If you type your final wishes on your computer, or if you scribble them on a hospital menu as you near death, or if you jot them down on the proverbial cocktail napkin, you have not created a will. To be valid, it must be prepared in strict accordance with certain formalities required by law.

First, the will needs to have been signed by the decedent (known as the "testator") in the presence of two witnesses.[1] All three people (testator and witnesses) need to sign in the presence of each other and in the presence of a notary public. Any adult who is mentally competent can be a witness. However, if one of the witnesses to a will is also a beneficiary of that will, then the gift to that person is void unless two other disinterested witnesses sign the will. (To be safe, the witnesses should be completely independent. They should not be family members or beneficiaries under the will.) The notary needs to sign a formal affidavit attesting to the manner of execution. If such an affidavit, known as a "self-proving affidavit," has not been signed, then one of the witnesses will need to testify in court as to the manner of execution of the will. Many a document that everyone thought was a will has not been honored by the courts because it failed to be signed with the proper formalities.

As long as you are mentally competent and not under duress, you can always revoke a will you have previously made. The laws of most states provide specific ways of revoking a will. In Massachusetts, for example, you can revoke your will and make a dramatic statement at the same time, by "burning, tearing, canceling, or obliterating it with the intention of

---

1   One of the authors remembers as a teenager having read a "Ripley's Believe It or Not" book in which a dead person signed a will. The story is as follows: The person died before signing his will. The disappointed heirs put a live fly in the dead person's mouth, put a pen in his hand, and guided the hand in making a signature. They were trying to meet the requirement of an old British statute which required that a will needed to be singed "while there is still life in the testator."

revoking it," or, with less fanfare, simply by making another will. (Massachusetts General Laws, Chapter 191, Section 8.) The law is similar in New Hampshire. If you prepare a will and then get divorced, the will remains valid, but any provision in it benefiting your ex-spouse is automatically revoked.

Most wills provide that the executor is to serve without bond, or with a minimum probate bond. Here, practice is dramatically different in New Hampshire and Massachusetts.

A probate bond is a type of insurance contract. In exchange for payment of a premium, the insurance company will make good any losses caused by the executor's dishonesty or theft of funds. In New Hampshire, even if the will directs that the executor serve without posting a bond, the Probate court will order that one be purchased. In Massachusetts, by contrast, the Probate court will honor the intent of the will, if the parties who are interested to the will so agree. In New Hampshire, the court will order that the amount of the bond be set proportionately to the size of the estate. Once the bond has been set, though, the court will typically allow the amount of the bond to be lowered, if all of the interested parties consent. This can be important, since the higher the amount of the bond, the more it costs. The bond premium is paid annually, and the bond must be renewed if the probate proceeding extends more than one year.

Although the Probate courts typically give the petitioner 30 days to purchase the bond, it is not unusual for the bonding process to take a good deal longer. Typically, the larger the amount of the bond, the longer the bonding process takes. Therefore, it is not unusual for the petitioner to seek an extension of time from the Probate court to purchase the bond. In recent years, insurance companies that issue probate bonds have become increasingly strict in their standards as to whom they will insure, and getting a probate bond is not always easy. This is especially true in large estates. Sometimes, people file probate petitions "pro se;" i.e., on their own, or without a lawyer. Purchasing a bond in these cases can be difficult, since sometimes bonding companies do not like to issue bonds without attorneys involved.

After the will has been accepted by the court and the bond has been purchased (if required), then the court formally appoints the executor by issuing a "certificate of appointment." This is an official document with the court seal, and gives the executor legal authority to act. One of the first duties of the executor is to notify the parties interested in the estate. New Hampshire and Massachusetts have somewhat different requirements in this regard, but, in essence, the idea is that anyone who is interested in the will or the estate has a right to know about the proceedings and the identity of the executor. Then, within three months of appointment, the executor makes an inventory of all of the assets to be probated, and reports that inventory, under oath, to the court. The inventory stays on file with the court and is a matter of public record.

If creditors have any claims against the estate, those claims are presented to the executor. A few years ago, the United States Supreme Court held that if an executor has knowledge of a creditor, (a credit card, for example) then he is required to notify the creditor that an estate has been opened. If the claim is valid, then the executor must pay it out of the decedent's assets. If the executor believes that the claim is not valid, then he notifies the creditor that the claim is being denied. It is then up to the creditor to decide whether to bring suit to enforce the claim. Of course, if the executor and creditor agree, the claim may be compromised, or settled. If there are any estate taxes due to either the state or the IRS, the executor, before closing the estate, needs to obtain a release from the relevant taxing authority, i.e., a document stating that all taxes are paid. At the end of the probate proceedings, before the assets can be distributed to the beneficiaries, the executor makes a report to the judge of all that he has done, as well as a report of the income and expenditures of the estate. This report is known as an "accounting." It is only after the judge approves of the accounting that the assets can be distributed to the heirs. The procedures for approval of an accounting are somewhat different in New Hampshire and Massachusetts, with New Hampshire having a more strict procedure.

In Massachusetts, if the assets to be probated do not exceed $15,000, plus a car, then full-fledged probate is not required. Rather, a simplified procedure known as "voluntary administration" is used. Under voluntary administration, there are fewer formalities and requirements than under regular probate administration. New Hampshire used to have a voluntary administration procedure, but the legislature abolished it a few years ago. Now, all estates in New Hampshire, regardless of size, are subject to the same basic probate procedures. However, unlike Massachusetts, New Hampshire has two procedures to simplify probate in certain cases.

Where the sole beneficiary of the will is a spouse or only child, and if that person is also nominated as executor, he or she may take advantage of "waiver of administration." Here, the court appoints the person as executor, and then has no further involvement. In other cases, assuming that all debts and taxes have been paid, and there are no objections or complications, then the executor may elect to use a procedure known as "summary administration." In a summary administration, if the just-mentioned requirements have been met, and if six months have passed since appointment of the executor, then the estate may be closed without additional court involvement.

Generally speaking, the advantage of probate is the court makes sure that the executor does what he or she is supposed to do. If not, the court can remove the executor. In the worst case, if the executor has misappropriated funds, the bonding company is supposed to pay. There are significant disadvantages of probate, though: publicity, delay, and expense. Probate is a public process. Your will is a public document, as is the probate inventory. Thus, who is inheriting what from your probate estate is a matter of public record. In these days, with increased dangers of fraud and identity theft, we question whether it is wise to make this financial information public. Also, wills are fairly easy to challenge. All legal heirs get notice of the estate and appointment of the executor, even heirs you might have wanted to disinherit or treat less favorably than others. This can lead to hard feelings and, in the worst case, a challenge to the will. Even if none of this occurs, you might want to keep your estate more private.

The second disadvantage of probate is the time involved. In Massachusetts, the process can easily take more than a year. In New Hampshire, this is also true, though the summary administration process described above has quickened many probates. However, even with summary administration, it can easily take nine months from the date of death until the court approves the motion for summary administration (closes the estate).

The final disadvantage of probate is the cost. While hiring an attorney is not required, it is certainly a sound idea, since an experienced attorney is trained in navigating the probate rules and laws. However, as we all know, attorneys can be quite expensive. The other cost of probate, in New Hampshire anyway, is the cost of the bond.

We believe that every person should have a "Pour-over Will," which is designed to work in conjunction with a trust. Trusts work perfectly to avoid probate, but they must be funded or filled with assets. This involves transferring title to real estate through new deeds and designation changes on bank accounts and certificates of deposit. Sometimes, however, clients accidentally forget to place something into their trust. In this case, the Pour-over Will operates to place, or "pour-over," that one omitted item into the trust.

B. The Revocable Trust as a Will Substitute

For the reasons set forth above, it is obvious why average folks want to spare their families from the probate process. Obviously, the delays, cost, and publicity of probate do not seem "optimum" to our clients. Those who wish to avoid probate for their families can take advantage of a trust. A key part of what we refer to as the Optimum Estate Plan is a Revocable Trust, also generally known as a "living trust," to serve as a substitute for a traditional will. In large part, the Revocable Trust says the same thing as a will, i.e., who is going to inherit the assets, and who will serve as the trustee (the functional equivalent of an executor).

The crucial difference between the Revocable Trust and a will, however, is the Revocable Trust is not subject to probate. The donor acts as sole trustee and manages the trust, taking out principal and interest for his use and enjoyment. Upon the donor's death, the "living trust" lives on with the donor's designated successor trustee (generally a spouse or children) wrapping up the trust in accordance with the donor's wishes. For this reason, the Revocable Trust avoids the delay, publicity, and expense that are involved in the probate process. A Revocable Trust is settled privately. Unlike the probate of a will, notice of which is published in the newspaper and in which all parties receive notice, trust administration requires no such procedures. You, the donor or "creator" of the Revocable Trust, control who is notified of the trust after your death. Thus, the general public has no access to it, and neither do any heirs or other people whom you do not wish to be notified. Second, a Revocable Trust can be settled quickly. Since a Revocable Trust does not go to probate, those time frames do not apply. In most cases, a Revocable Trust can be settled in a few weeks.

Consider the hypothetical of two individuals, John and Henry, who happen to die on the same day. John had his assets in a Revocable Trust, and Henry had a traditional will. It would not be unusual for John's trust to be completely settled and the money distributed even before the court has appointed the executor of Henry's will. While Henry's beneficiaries are just getting started, John's beneficiaries are already enjoying their inheritance. Finally, since a Revocable Trust avoids probate, the trustee does not have to hire an attorney in order to settle it. Thus, a Revocable Trust can be settled far more economically than a will. Years ago, it was mainly the wealthy who prepared Revocable Trusts, while most other people simply prepared wills. These days, Revocable Trusts have become standard estate-planning tools for people of moderate means.

C. The Revocable Trust – Minimizing Estate Taxes for Married Couples

The majority of our clients are folks of average means, and minimization or elimination of estate taxes is generally not their concern. Probate avoidance and loss of life savings due to a prolonged nursing-home stay are their concern. For that reason, it is not our intention to spend much time on sophisticated estate-planning techniques used by rich people. However, where appropriate, the use of two Revocable Trusts is the "optimum" method for a married couple to legally avoid or minimize estate taxes.

This only comes into play on the federal level for married clients with assets in excess of $2 million, which is scheduled to "roll-back" to $1 million in the year 2011. However, the state of Massachusetts currently has an estate tax that renders taxable estates of $1 million or more. In reaching these amounts, all assets owned by a married couple—including IRAs, the fair market value of its real estate and life-insurance proceeds—must be included. If a married couple has combined assets of more than the stated amounts, it can, through the use of two trusts, pass to their heirs twice the amount listed above. For example, let's look at the married couple we'll call Jim and Jane. Generally put, upon Jim's death, Jane takes over as trustee of Jim's trust and can distribute the funds to herself. In addition, a provision is usually inserted that the trustee may, in the discretion of such successor spouse-trustee, make distributions of income or principal to their children for their health, maintenance, support, and education.

D. Special Nursing Home Issues

Whether you opt for a will or a Revocable Trust in your estate plan, you must be very careful if your spouse is ill or needs nursing-home care. Naturally, most wills and trusts for married couples leave all of the assets to the surviving spouse. If your spouse is a permanent resident of a nursing home, or likely to become one after your death, however, you may want to think twice about automatically naming that spouse as beneficiary.

Let's say that your spouse is in a nursing home and receiving Medicaid benefits. You have a will or trust that leaves everything to your spouse. If you die prior to your spouse, then all of the assets will go to him or her. He or she will immediately lose Medicaid coverage, and will have to spend down the inheritance. It is likely that the children will receive nothing. To avoid this situation, you could have amended your estate-planning documents to say that if you die first, your assets would pass to your children instead of your ill spouse. You may also want to amend the beneficiary designations on your life insurance and IRAs in the same way. Of course, you are free to leave your assets to your spouse if you want, but in our experience, most people would rather have the inheritance go to the children, instead of to the nursing home.

Chapter 3
Durable Financial
Powers Of Attorney

*A*nother crucial document in the Optimum Estate Plan is the Durable Financial Power of Attorney. Consider this very common situation, which we encounter often in our estate-planning practice.

Betty and Bob have been married for 45 years. For most of their lives, Bob was the primary breadwinner, and by the time he retired, his 401k was worth $450,000. When Betty and Bob were busy working and raising their children, they did not pay much attention to estate planning, and, after they retired, were too busy traveling, playing golf, and spoiling the grandchildren to attend to business. One day, Bob has a stroke, which leaves him unable to manage his affairs. Betty needs to access Bob's 401k, but she has never really paid attention to it before, and doesn't know much about it. However, she manages to find the papers and calls the brokerage house that is holding the money.

She tells the representative she is Bob's wife, and that she needs to take some money from the account to pay bills. The person she speaks to gives her the bad news: he is unable to help her, since the money belongs to Bob. Not only does Betty not have any authority to access the funds, but she is not even entitled to any information about the account. Betty gets the same story when she calls the company that holds Bob's life insurance and stock account. Betty has been stymied because she and Bob never signed Durable Powers of Attorney.

The story gets even worse. Say Bob's condition declines and he needs care in a nursing home. As we will see in a later chapter, Betty can save just about all of the money if she puts it into the proper type of immediate annuity for her benefit. However, not having a Power of Attorney, she hits the same brick wall. Without the proper legal documentation, she is stuck. She will have to petition the Probate court for guardianship, which is a drawn-out, expensive, and emotionally painful process.

As we have seen with the example of Bob, which unfortunately is quite common, someone who has become incompetent does not have the legal capacity to transact business, such as paying bills, signing tax returns, buying or selling property, or making contracts. When an incompetent person has not signed a Durable Power of Attorney, someone such as a spouse, adult child, or other interested party must petition the Probate court to become guardian over the estate. The procedure for obtaining guardianship is similar in New Hampshire and Massachusetts, though there are differences.

To obtain guardianship in New Hampshire, you have to prove to the court's satisfaction that the person cannot take care of his or her financial or business affairs. The court will hold a hearing, and you will have to present specific testimony and evidence to convince the judge that the person cannot handle these matters, and is endangered thereby. All evidence needs to be dated within the past six months, and at least one example needs to be within the past 20 days. The ward has an opportunity to rebut your evidence and present contrary evidence of his own. The ward has an absolute right to counsel, and, if he cannot afford an attorney, one will be provided by the state. If you believe that it would be harmful for the ward to attend the hearing, or if the ward has no capability of understanding what the hearing is about, then you need to present an affidavit to that effect from the ward's physician, and the court needs to formally excuse the ward's attendance.

If you do convince the court because of lack of sufficient proof for a guardian, then the court will carefully limit your authority to powers that are needed, and no more. As we have seen, New Hampshire law and the Probate courts scrupulously safeguard the ward's rights and liberties.

Where the guardianship concerns money or property (guardianship over the estate), the court will order that the guardian post a bond, file an inventory under oath, and make a full financial accounting once a year. The court staff reviews the guardian's accounts in detail, and holds guardians to an exacting, precise standard of reporting and conduct. Where the guardianship concerns issues like medical decision-making and living arrangements (guardianship over the person), then the guardian is required to make an annual report to the court as to the ward's health, condition, and living arrangements. If the guardian needs to sell some of the ward's assets to pay bills, for example, prior court approval is needed, and, after the sale, an accounting of the proceeds will be required.

The process in Massachusetts, by contrast, is archaic, sorely in need of overhaul, and does much less to protect the rights of the ward. In Massachusetts, wards are pigeonholed into the outmoded categories of "mentally ill," "mentally retarded," "spendthrifts," and "persons unable to make or communicate informed decisions." There is no right to counsel on the part of the ward, and only medical evidence is required, frequently in the form of an affidavit only. The state laws do not even specify what type of medical evidence is needed. Thus, if the ward wishes to contest the guardianship, he does not know the type of evidence to be presented against him, or what type of contrary evidence is required by him.

On January 13, 2008, The Boston Globe published an article, "Courts Strip Elders of Their Independence." The Globe did a review of the Suffolk County Probate and Family Court, and wrote a scathing critique of the process. In large part, the Globe found that the court approved guardianship petitions far too quickly, giving just minimal protection of the rights of wards. According to the article:

"Too many judges ... award custody of elders to guardians without insisting on the minimal medical documentation required by court rules; without asking about the patient's long term prognosis; and without considering whether an independent fact finder should conduct an inquiry before such a life altering judgment is rendered. And those whose lives are so radically affected are given no legal representation." The article went on to say:

"After the court declares someone mentally ill and appoints a guardian, for all practical purposes most of the patients officially vanish. Almost none of the state's probate courts have any mechanism to track their whereabouts, monitor their treatment, determine whether they have recovered enough to reclaim their freedom and autonomy, or even learn whether they are dead or alive.

Handcuffed by an antiquated computer system, the courts know how many cases are filed but do not know how many people judges put under the control of guardians each year. The number in Massachusetts each year almost certainly exceeds 2,000.

Virtually unregulated, guardians, many of them lawyers and social workers, regularly ignore requirements that they file an initial inventory of assets of the people they are responsible for and an annual accounting of how they managed a person's finances. In Suffolk Probate Court, where five years of guardianship filings were examined, there were no financial reports in 85 percent of the cases."

We have not made an independent study of the Globe's findings and are not able to take a position as to the accuracy of the article. However, we are able to state that New Hampshire is far ahead of Massachusetts in terms of efficiency and protection of the rights of the ward.

The benefits of guardianship are that the court oversees what the guardian does (at least in New Hampshire) and the guardian must be bonded. On the other hand, there are significant drawbacks to guardianship. It is time-consuming, expensive, cumbersome, and emotionally painful for the family. Expenses include attorney's fees for the petitioner and the ward, and the cost of the bond. The bond must be renewed and paid for annually. Typically, there is a court fee for filing a motion and an annual account. Frequently, attorneys or accountants prepare annual accounts, and, of course, these professionals must be paid. A guardian must file an inventory of the assets, and typically pay an attorney to prepare this document. There is an emotional cost, as well, to guardianship, in that you need to bring an adversarial court proceeding against a close family member, and have attorneys and the legal system get involved with your family's private affairs. Finally, guardianship is cumbersome. You need to obtain court permission to sell any assets and to do estate planning for the ward. If the ward goes into a nursing home and you want to shelter assets, you will be stymied. Obviously, every case is different. In general, though, we believe that most people would be better off to structure their affairs to avoid guardianship.

The Optimum Estate Plan avoids guardianship proceedings by including a document known as a "Durable Power of Attorney." If you become incompetent, the holder of your DPOA (called the "Attorney-in-Fact," or agent) can transact your business for you, much as a guardian would do, without reporting to the Probate court or going through any of the probate formalities. Thus, the court hearing, Medical Certificate (in Massachusetts), attorneys, bond, and accounting are all avoided. The family's financial affairs are kept within the family and without any involvement by the legal system. If you insert Medicaid planning provisions in the DPOA, (discussed in later chapters), then the Attorney-in-Fact would be able to shelter assets for you.

The basic Durable Power of Attorney document is similar in New Hampshire and Massachusetts. There is an itemized list of things that the Attorney-in-Fact is able to do, such as:

1. Engage in banking transactions.
2. Collect debts owed to the principal, or pay debts owed by the principal.
3. Buy and sell real estate and personal property.
4. Use the principal's funds for his health, welfare, and support.

5. Register and title motor vehicles.
6. Rent a new safe deposit box, or enter an existing one.
7. Employ agents, accountants, attorneys, or any one else do the principal's business.
8. Make gifts, if doing so would be consistent with the principal's tax objectives or to shelter assets from long-term care.
9. Deal with the IRS and similar retirement plans.

In fact, a Power of Attorney can be as formal or informal as the parties' desire, and can be customized to meet the situation. Usually, each spouse names the other as Attorney-in-Fact, with one of the children as a backup. Single people typically name one of the children, with a second child as a backup. The Power of Attorney can be effective immediately, or it can become effective upon a doctor's certification that you have become unable to manage your financial affairs. However you structure it, though, the key is it allows a trusted person to manage your finances without court involvement. It is important to know that a Power of Attorney is automatically terminated on the death of the principal.

The format of the Durable Power of Attorney is very similar for New Hampshire and Massachusetts. The one big difference concerns a document known as a "disclosure statement." That is, in New Hampshire, each Durable Power of Attorney must have attached two disclosure statements: one signed by the principal and one signed by the agent. The principal's statement is a reminder to him that the agent has broad powers, and essentially is a warning that the principal needs to have the utmost faith and confidence in the person he appoints as agent. The agent needs to sign a statement that explains he owes the highest duties of care, faith, and loyalty to the principal, and that he must at all times act in the best interests of the principal.

In either state, you can revoke a Durable Power of Attorney at any time. In either New Hampshire or Massachusetts, you can empower your agent to try to shelter your assets in the event you need nursing-home care. The ability to do this is one very distinct advantage of a Durable Power of Attorney over guardianship. In Massachusetts, guardians can engage in Medicaid planning with permission of the court, but this is a cumbersome process, and there is no guarantee that the court will approve. In New Hampshire, it is almost a certainty that the court will not approve any petition by a guardian to protect the ward's assets from nursing home spend-down.

Those with IRAs, 401ks, or similar retirement accounts have a particular need for a Durable Power of Attorney. Recall the case of Bob and Betty, discussed at the beginning of this chapter. Bob had become incapacitated, and Betty needed to have access to his IRA. In recent years, IRA and 401k custodians have become increasingly strict in requiring specific language in the Durable Power of Attorney that authorizes the agent to deal with retirement accounts. Since these firms only started to impose this requirement fairly recently, anyone who has such accounts, and who has a Durable Power of Attorney that is more than four or five years old, should consider having it done again to include the required language.

Chapter 4
Advance Directives:
Living Wills and
Medical Powers of Attorney

*L*et's return to our friends Bob and Betty. When Bob had his stroke, he was taken by ambulance to the emergency room. Betty was not home at the time, and when she found out what had happened, she rushed to the hospital. She asked the doctors how Bob was doing, but they did not give her any information. Stunned, Betty, in tears, protested that she was Bob's wife, but the doctors were unrelenting. Near hysteria, she did not now know what to do and feared the worst. Fortunately, Bob regained consciousness, and gave the doctors permission to speak to Betty.

What happened here? A law known as the Health Insurance Portability and Accountability Act of 1996 (HIPAA) has prevented Bob's doctors from talking to Betty. According to the Centers for Medicare and Medicaid Services web site, "The Administrative Simplification provisions of the Health Insurance Portability and Accountability Act of 1996 (HIPAA, Title II) required the Department of Health and Human Services (DHHS) to establish national standards for electronic health care transactions and national identifiers for providers, health plans, and employers. It also addressed the security and privacy of health data."

Due to the privacy regulations enacted under the law, Bob's doctors could not talk to Betty without Bob's permission. In our experience, the HIPAA law has caused families a great deal of trouble, since doctors will not talk to spouses or adult children. We have even seen cases in which doctors' offices would not let one spouse make medical appointments for another spouse. No one will dispute that protecting medical information is an admirable goal, but it seems that the law has gone too far.

In any event, had Bob and Betty had the Optimum Estate Plan, they would have avoided this problem, because it includes documents known as "Advance Directives." In New Hampshire, an Advance Directive includes a Health Care Power of Attorney and a Living Will. In Massachusetts, an Advance Directive is limited to a Health Care Proxy. The Medical Power of Attorney or Health Care Proxy, as the case may be, allows your spouse, children, or other trusted person you name to receive otherwise confidential medical information and make medical decisions if you cannot. If you become incompetent and do not have a Medical Power of Attorney, (like Bob), your family would need to seek a court guardianship, and, until the guardianship is approved, would not be able to get medical information. Clearly, signing the Medical Power of Attorney will avoid lengthy and potentially costly court proceedings in a time of crisis. Medical Powers of Attorney/Health Care Proxies are standard forms, available at hospitals and senior citizens centers. Of course, any client who puts in place the Optimum Estate Plan will have such a document.

Most readers will recall the case of Terri Schiavo. This unfortunate young woman suffered irreversible brain damage and became dependent on a feeding tube. She was in a persistent vegetative state and was in a nursing home for 15 years. In 1998, her husband, Michael Schiavo, who was also her guardian, asked the court for authority to remove her feeding tube. Terri's parents opposed him. Although the lower court found that Terri would not wish to continue life prolonging measures, the appeals lasted for seven years. There was international news coverage, and even Congress got involved. Ultimately, in March 2005, the feeding tube was removed and she died at age 41. The seven-year court battle was completely preventable. The basic problem was that Terri did not execute an Advance Directive during her life. The absence of this document allowed her husband to argue to the courts that Terri would not have wanted heroic measures to prolong a certain death, and at the same time allowed her parents to argue the opposite. The truth about her opinion, if indeed she had an opinion, will never be known.

Obviously, her case was tragic. She was stricken at a young age and languished in nursing homes for more than a decade. Beyond that, though, her family was torn apart and fortunes were spent on pointless legal battles. The further tragedy was that it was all preventable. Had Terri only executed an Advance Directive, her wishes would have been known, and the medical system would have been legally bound to carry out those wishes. Whether or not you believe in heroic, end-of-life matters is an intensely personal affair, and there is no right or wrong. What is definitely wrong, though, is to leave your loved ones in the dark about what you want.

Chapter 5
The Medicaid Rules in General

*T*hese days, a long-term nursing home stay can spell financial disaster for most people. The annual cost of a typical nursing home is $90,000 to $100,000. Very few people can withstand these costs for very long before getting wiped out. Although there are some "protections" for married couples, they are meager and can easily lead to a life of poverty or near poverty for a healthy spouse. To explain how the "Optimum Estate Plan" can work to alleviate the financial devastation caused by a prolonged nursing-home stay, it is necessary to start at the beginning with a discussion of how nursing homes in this country are financed.

A. The Difference Between Medicare and Medicaid

Medicare is the basic health-insurance program available to anyone who is disabled or over 65 and has paid into the Social Security system. Many people believe that Medicare pays for long-term nursing home care. However, people who believe this and who later enter a nursing home are in for a very unpleasant and expensive surprise, since Medicare is not designed to cover long-term nursing home care. If a Medicare beneficiary spends three nights in the hospital and then goes to a nursing home for rehabilitation, Medicare will pay the nursing home in full for the first 20 days, and then in part from day 21 to 100. However, once the patient stops making improvement, Medicare and the Medicare supplement stop paying, even if this occurs before expiration of the 100 days. Thus, Medicare for skilled nursing care is meant to be a short-term benefit only. People who need long-term nursing home care are not covered.

B. Three Ways of Paying for Nursing Homes

Since Medicare will not cover long-term care, what will? There are three ways to pay for a nursing home: long-term care insurance, private payment, and Medicaid.[2]

1. Long-Term Care Insurance

Long-term care insurance is a type of health insurance that will pay for prolonged nursing-home stays, provided that the conditions of the insurance policy are met. Depending on the policy, payment can be for as little as two years, or for as long as a lifetime. The insurance can pay anywhere from a

---

2 According to the Federal Centers for Medicare & Medicaid Services, for the years 1980 to 2003, Medicaid paid 46.0% of nursing home costs, private funds paid for 27.9%, Medicare paid for 12.4%, private insurance paid for 7.7% and other sources paid 6.1%. See Centers for Medicare and Medicaid Services, Nat'l. Health Expenditures by Type of Service and Source of Funds, Calendar Years 1980-03, quoted in E. O'Brien, "Medicaid's Coverage of Nursing Home Costs: Asset Shelter for the Wealthy or Essential Safety Net," Georgetown University, May 2005, p. 1.

minimal amount of the nursing-home charges all the way to payment in full. The better policies come with an "inflation rider," which means that the policy benefit rises each year. Some policies also include payment for home health care. Since nursing-home insurance decreases people's reliance on Medicaid, the government is enacting policies that encourage people to buy this insurance. Under federal law, for example, the premiums for certain long-term care policies are deductible in part as a medical expense. In Massachusetts, if you have a long-term care policy that pays at least $125 per day for two years, and if you enter a nursing home and eventually receive Medicaid assistance, the state will not make a claim against your estate at your death.

Unfortunately, for two reasons, long-term care insurance is not a one-size-fits-all solution. First, it is simply too expensive for most senior citizens to afford, especially in this age of low interest rates, rising medical costs, gasoline, heating prices, and grocery prices. Second, not everyone qualifies for the insurance. Insurance companies set standards for the people they will insure, and, depending on a person's health, he or she might not qualify. In our view, this is a significant shortcoming of the system. If the government is discouraging the use of asset protection strategies, and is encouraging the use of long-term care insurance, then it makes no sense to allow insurance companies to set premiums that most people cannot afford and impose underwriting standards that most people cannot meet. Our national leaders of both political parties have failed completely to adequately address the problem of long-term care financing.

2. Private Payment

Since relatively few people have long-term care insurance, most people who enter the nursing home begin by paying privately. The problem, of course, is that nursing homes are extremely expensive. Costs of $8,000 to $9,000 a month are common. When the money runs out, nursing home residents are forced to turn to the next method of payment, which is Medicaid.

3. Medicaid

Medicaid is a government program that is administered by the states pursuant to federal requirements. It pays for medical treatment and room and board at the nursing home when you have run out of funds. In Massachusetts, Medicaid is also known as Mass Health. For the remainder of this book, the term "Medicaid" will refer both to the New Hampshire and Massachusetts versions of the program. The laws surrounding Medicaid are very similar in both states, and we will point out any differences.

3A. Applying for Medicaid

In order to qualify for Medicaid, you must meet certain medical and financial requirements. First, you must either live in a nursing home or have a medical need that requires care in one. In New Hampshire, applications for Medicaid benefits are filed with the Medicaid District Office covering the geographical area in which you live. In Massachusetts, applications are filed at one of four "enrollment centers," located in Tewksbury, Revere, Taunton, and Springfield. In New Hampshire, after an application is received, the district office will schedule a personal interview, during which the case technician will go over the documentation that was submitted with the application. In Massachusetts, there is no personal interview, and all communication is done by mail. The enrollment center will mail out a document known as an "information request." This is a questionnaire calling for production of any missing documentation, and explanation of any documents that the caseworker has questions about.

In either state, proper documentation, known as "verifications," is the key to filing a successful Medicaid application. At a minimum, you will have to provide the following verifications:

1. Residence – Copy of deed or lease.
2. Age and Citizenship – Copy of birth or baptismal certificate, naturalization certificate, or green card.
3. Social Security, Medicare and private health insurance cards. If there is a private health insurance, then a copy of the latest bill will also be required.
4. Marriage certificate, for married applicants.
5. Current bank account statements, and frequently, checking statements going back one year and some times three years. You will need to explain and document any large or unusual withdrawals.
6. Statement of nursing home personal-needs account.
7. Life insurance policies and statement of cash value for all policies that have a combined face value of $1,500 or more.
8. Copy of Durable Power of Attorney.
9. All trust documents along with verification of all assets in the trust name.

10. Pre-paid burial contract and cemetery deed.
11. Verification of all other financial assets such as stocks, bonds, mutual funds, etc. and the value thereof.
12. Copies of any annuity contracts.
13. Verification of any assets transferred within the 60 months. This requirement applies to gifts and any asset sold within the relevant time frame. In the case of a house sale, for example, a closing statement will be required as well as proof of deposit on the closing proceeds. The spend-down of these proceeds will also have to be accounted for.
14. Verification of all income, such as Social Security award statements and pension check stubs. For income that is directly deposited, a bank statement will do.
15. If bank accounts or other assets have been closed in the past five years, an accounting of the proceeds of the proceeds of these accounts.

Providing these verifications can be the most tedious and difficult part the application process. However, it is of the utmost importance, as an application will not be approved until all verifications have been provided and all issues raised by the verifications have been explained. The burden of providing the verifications is on the applicant; the Medicaid office will not assist you in getting these documents.

In recent years, both New Hampshire and Massachusetts have become ever so strict, sometimes to the point of harassment, in enforcing this requirement. A client of ours was once involved in a Medicaid application in Massachusetts in which the case technician wanted explanations of routine ATM withdrawals. Recently in New Hampshire, the Medicaid Office insisted upon finding out what assets had funded the applicant's trust some 16 years earlier. One Medicaid application in which we were involved was denied because of failure to produce documents; the problem we had with this is that the caseworker never bothered to request the documents that were not produced. Horror stories such as these do happen.

There are fairly tight deadlines in providing the verifications, and failing to meet them means verifications will be denied. For this reason, we advise you assemble the verifications before filing the application, and to make sure that those verifications are complete. For example, most bank statements contain two to five pages. Often, one or two of these pages do not contain any useful information, such as a cover page that doesn't say anything or a blank form so you can balance the account. Nevertheless, all of these pages need to be produced.

In New Hampshire, while most Medicaid case technicians try to be helpful and understanding, the interview and application process is lengthy and frequently grueling. Many clients go through the process and later feel they have been treated like criminals, or put on trial. A caseworker who will not be identified told one of us that they are trained to assume that all applicants are lying and withholding information, and to treat them accordingly. As of this writing, it is not unusual for the State of New Hampshire to take five to seven months before issuing a Medicaid decision, in complete violation of law. During the time that the applications have been pending, clients have begun to report that nursing homes have been after them for payment. In Massachusetts, by contrast, applications are typically handled in a timely and efficient manner.

Under federal law, a Medicaid application can seek payments retroactive to the three months prior to the application filing. However, since the application process itself can take two to three months, and sometimes longer (not usually the case in Massachusetts, but routine in New Hampshire), Since the nursing home is not being paid while the application is pending, you would be well advised to start the process before running out of money, rather than after.

It is of the utmost importance to be accurate and truthful on the application, since any willful misrepresentation can be prosecuted as fraud. The question typically arises as to what happens if you make a statement on the application that you believe to be true, but later, information turns up that shows the information is false. A similar issue arises when you disclose your assets, and then later discover assets you did not know about. If you were honest when you filed the application, and if you promptly report the new information to the caseworker, then you are not in any trouble at all. The key, however, is to promptly report the change you have discovered. In the case where assets are discovered that you did not know about, you will come off Medicaid, and the assets will need to be spent down. When the assets have been spent down, you will qualify for Medicaid again.

If you are dissatisfied with the results of the application, you can request an appeal, known as a "fair hearing." The fair hearing is not a second chance, but a proceeding at which you will have to prove that the caseworker wrongfully denied the application due to a mistake of fact, or a mistake in applying the law. Fair hearings are conducted by a hearings examiner, who is an employee of the state or the Medicaid agency.   At a fair hearing, each side will have the ability to offer evidence and state the legal basis of his or her case.   Although the testimony is taken under oath, and witnesses are subject to cross-examination, and the proceedings are far less formal than those of a court room.   The process of claiming a fair hearing is simple and informal. Usually, a letter to the Medicaid caseworker who handled the application will suffice.   However, there are strict deadlines for doing so.   Unfortunately, in New Hampshire at least, it can take up to nine months to get a decision from the hearings examiner after the hearing is conducted.

Under Federal law, a nursing home cannot discriminate, discharge, or in any way alter the treatment of a Medicaid patient.   If, shortly before a private-pay patient switches to Medicaid, the facility transfers the patient to a hospital or to another part of the facility, you have cause to investigate and determine whether the move was medically justified.   Additionally, any facility that accepts federal funds, such as Medicare or Medicaid, has no legal right to require that other family members contribute to the payment or guarantee payment. Any contracts providing such guarantees are void.

3B. Medicaid's Financial Requirements General Rules

Medicaid law puts very strict limits on the amount and type of assets that a recipient is allowed to have.   Certain types of assets are not counted towards eligibility, and, accordingly, are called "non-countable assets," whereas certain assets are countable.   You are allowed to have unlimited non-countable assets, but there are limits on the countable assets you may have.   Non-countable assets include, among others:

- Your home, provided that the healthy or "community" spouse is living there (or certain limited classes of relatives are living there). Note that only one residence is exempt, so that if you have a vacation home, investment property, or second home, the non-homestead property will be countable. As we will see later on, there are now limits as to how much the house can be worth.

• Pre-paid funeral contracts, as long as they are irrevocable, i.e., you do not have the right to cancel the contract for a refund. Some states have limits on the amount that can be paid for the funeral. Note that the payment must be for the cost of the funeral. That is, you cannot "over pay" for the funeral, and then get a refund of any unused amounts afterwards. In Massachusetts, you can also have a $1,500 bank account earmarked for burial expenses.

• One burial plot for the applicant and spouse.

• Essential household items, such as appliances, clothing, household furnishings, and personal, non-investment jewelry.

• Property subject to legal proceedings, such as property in probate.

• Lump sum death benefits for funeral and burial expenses.

• Income tax refunds.

• One motor vehicle. Some states put a cap on the value of the vehicle.

• Cash value of life-insurance policies, up to $1,500. Insurance is only exempt if the face value is below $1,500. If the face value exceeds $1,500, then the cash value is added up, and only $1,500 is exempt. In New Hampshire, the cash value of all life insurance is counted as an asset.

- Term life insurance, with no cash value.
- Cash assets up to $2,000 in Massachusetts and $2,500 in New Hampshire.

All other assets are countable, with no exceptions. Examples of countable assets are bank accounts, IRAs, and similar retirement accounts, cash value of life insurance above $1,500, stocks, bonds, mutual funds, second homes, second cars, deferred annuities, and anything else of whatever kind or description that can be sold or turned into cash.

If you have countable assets over the allowable limit, you will not be eligible for Medicaid until you have "spent down" to the limit. This process will be discussed later. Alternatively, and the very point of this book, is that there are certain, very powerful Medicaid planning devices that you can use to preserve most your countable assets and will still allow you to qualify for Medicaid.

Medicaid has separate rules for income. In the case of a single person, all of the income, with certain exceptions, must be paid to the nursing home. You are allowed to keep a minimal "personal needs allowance" of no more than $60 per month, as well as sufficient money to pay for health insurance premiums. In the case of a married couple, the income of the healthy spouse is not counted, while the income of the institutionalized spouse is. The healthy spouse does have the benefit of certain income protections, discussed below.

4. Division of Assets for Married Couples

Under a law ironically known as the "Spousal Impoverishment" provisions of the Medicare Catastrophic Coverage Act of 1988, the healthy spouse benefits from certain, albeit minimal, asset protections. Unfortunately, these protections can hardly be called that at all. In Medicaid parlance, the spouse in a nursing home is known as the "institutionalized spouse," and the spouse living at home is known as the "community spouse." Congress, in passing the Spousal Impoverishment law, recognized that it would not be in society's interest to completely impoverish the community spouse. In New Hampshire, the community spouse is allowed to keep half of the couple's countable assets, or $104,400, whichever is less. In Massachusetts, the community spouse is allowed to keep the first $104,400.

It makes no difference whose name the assets are in, and it makes no difference who brought the asset to the marriage. Many spouses, especially those involved in second marriages, take false comfort in that their assets are in separate names, or from the fact that they have entered into a pre-marital agreement. When a spouse in a second marriage enters a nursing home, however, the community spouse is in for an extremely uncomfortable surprise: whose name the asset is in, or whether there is a pre-marital agreement, is completely irrelevant. When couples say "I do," they are, for Medicaid purposes, consenting to treat their assets as if they were jointly held. In the eyes of the law, the marital unit has one pocketbook.

The "protection" provided by the Spousal Impoverishment law is not automatic; it must be requested by the community spouse in a procedure known as a "resource assessment." Once the institutionalized spouse enters a hospital, skilled or intermediate nursing facility and is likely to remain institutionalized for 30 consecutive days or more, the community spouse is entitled to have the resource assessment done. The resource assessment does not have to be done at that time; it can be done later, as part of the Medicaid application itself and after the spend-down has taken place. However, the community spouse would be well advised to do the resource assessment as early as possible. Because the resource assessment is essentially a financial "snapshot" of the assets on the date of institutionalization, it is easier to get the needed financial records shortly after the fact, rather than months or sometimes years later. The documentation required to process a resource assessment is the same as that needed for a full application.

The mechanics of a resource assessment are as follows. The value of all countable assets are added, and divided by two. The result is called the "spousal share." In New Hampshire, for couples with assets of up to approximately $50,000, the community spouse may keep the entire amount rather than half of the total. For those coupes with assets above $50,000, the community spouse in New Hampshire may keep half, up to a cap of $104,400. As mentioned above, in Massachusetts the community spouse can keep the first $104,400.

5. Treatment of Income for Married Couples

How does Medicaid treat income? Once the asset tests have been met, the state will then consider the income of the married couple. Subject to deductions for the personal-needs allowance and medical insurance, the income of the institutionalized spouse must be paid to the nursing home in full. However, depending on the couple's circumstances, the community spouse may be allowed to keep some of the income of the institutionalized spouse, instead of this income being paid to the nursing home. Under federal law, each state must establish a "Minimum Monthly Maintenance Needs Allowance" (MMMNA). The MMMNA must be at least 150 percent of the federal poverty line for a family of two, and it rises each year. Currently, the MMMNA is $1,711.25, and the maximum is $2,610.

If the community spouse's income is below the MMMNA, he will be entitled to an "allowance" from the income of the institutionalized spouse. There is formula set by the federal government to establish the spousal income allowance. There are two ways, using Medicaid planning techniques, of raising the community spouse's monthly income allowance. First, the community spouse can request a fair hearing, claiming financial distress. In Massachusetts, there is a complex way of raising the community spouse asset allowance if, after getting an income allowance from the institutionalized spouse, the income of the community spouse is below the MMMNA. Alternatively, he or she can seek a court order of support against the institutionalized spouse. If the court finds that the community spouse is entitled to higher income, then the court order would supersede the amount that the state Medicaid agency determined.

6. The Spend-down

Due to Medicaid's strict asset limits, many people need to "spend down" their assets in order to qualify for benefits. If you need to do this, there are certain spend-down strategies that can help you. As mentioned above, certain assets are not countable for Medicaid purposes. It is perfectly permissible to spend money on non-countable assets, as long as you pay fair value for them. For example, a pre-paid funeral contract is not a countable asset. In this way, the funeral is paid for out of the spend-down funds, i.e., the funds that would otherwise have gone to the nursing home, and not the funds protected for the community spouse. One car per family is also not countable. Therefore, the community spouse can trade in the old car and buy a new one. He or she can also buy furniture, personal items, perform home improvements and repairs, or pay down bills. Care should be taken, however, not to buy items, such as expensive jewelry, artwork, or a luxury car, as these items may be considered to be investments, which would then be countable.

Whether assets are liquidated by making purchases or by paying the nursing home (obviously the last resort), attention must be given to the tax consequences of the spend-down. Many people today hold the bulk of their wealth in retirement assets such as IRAs and 401ks. While the income tax treatment of these assets is beyond the scope of this book, there are significant income tax consequences when these assets are liquidated. The same is true of appreciated assets such as stocks and real estate, and assets with a taxable component, such as savings bonds and annuities. Therefore, it is very often advisable to consult with an accountant or financial advisor prior to finalizing plans as to the order in which assets should be liquidated.

Spending down in accordance with the state requirements, however, can be viewed as a last resort. We have already seen some modest techniques that can minimize what you and your spouse have to spend. The field of Medicaid planning, which we discuss in later chapters, can actually allow you to save the bulk of your wealth—sometimes all of it—while making you eligible for Medicaid.

Chapter 6
The Medicaid Transfer of Asset Rules and the Deficit Reduction Act

*I*n order to have a complete understanding of Medicaid law, and how the Optimum Estate Plan works to minimize Medicaid spend-down, you must be familiar with the transfer-of-asset rules. These rules changed significantly with the Deficit Reduction Act (DRA), effective February 8, 2006. In order to understand the DRA, it is essential to understand the pre-DRA law.

Under the pre-DRA transfer-of-asset rules, if a gift or transfer of assets is made for less than fair market value within three (or sometimes five) years of applying for Medicaid. Then the donor (maker) of the gift will be disqualified for Medicaid benefits. The length of the disqualification will increase with the size of the gift. More precisely, the length of the disqualification will be equal to the size of the gift, divided by the average private-pay nursing home rate in the state (the "disqualification rate"). The idea is that if you gave away sufficient assets to pay for, say, six months in the nursing home, then you will be unable to qualify for Medicaid benefits for six months. If you give away sufficient assets to pay for one year, you will be disqualified for one year, and so on. So, if the disqualification rate is $7,000 per month, and if you give away $70,000 on January 1, they you will be disqualified from Medicaid benefits for 10 months, or until November 1.

The transfer-of-asset rule tied into another Medicaid concept: the "look-back period." Under the pre-DRA rules, there was a 36-month look-back period for transfers of assets to individuals, and a 60-month look-back period for transfers to Irrevocable Trusts. That is, Medicaid can only ask about, or "look back" on, transfers that have occurred within the past 36 months, or 60 months to an Irrevocable Trust. If you gave away a $100,000 asset to your son 37 months ago, Medicaid will not take the gift into account because the gift fell outside of the look-back period. However, if you gave a $70,000 asset to your son within the 36-month look-back period, then you will be disqualified from Medicaid for 10 months in a state in which the transfer divisor is $7,000 per month.

In these circumstances, a transfer of the home was not penalized. There are certain exceptions to the transfer-of-asset rules that pertained to the family home.

- To avoid foreclosure.
- To a spouse or to a child who is blind or permanently or totally disabled.
- To an adult child who has lived in the house and provided care to the parent, such that the parent was kept out of the nursing home for two years.

- To a sibling who has an equity interest in the home, and who resided there for at least one year prior to the individual's admission to the nursing home.

Under pre-DRA law, gift planning was fairly straightforward. Using our example of $70,000, you could safely gift that amount if you retained sufficient assets to pay for the next 10 months in the nursing home. Or, say your total assets were $140,000, and you went into the nursing home on January 1. You could give away $70,000, be disqualified for 10 months, and use your remaining $70,000 to pay for the following 10 months.

The DRA, however, has drastically tightened these rules. First, the Medicaid look-back period for all asset transfers is now five years. Previously, only Irrevocable Trusts carried a five-year look-back period.

Under pre-DRA law, the Medicaid disqualification period for transferred assets started from the date of transfer. As long as the disqualification period was over, then, all things being equal, Medicaid would be approved. The new law states that the disqualification period runs not from the date of the gift, but from the date when the individual enters a nursing home and would otherwise be eligible for Medicaid coverage. In other words, the penalty period does not even begin until the nursing-home resident is out of funds and has applied for Medicaid.

Two simple examples will show how these rules work, using a hypothetical disqualification rate of $7,000.

Let's assume that Uncle Harry gives away $70,000 on January 1, 2008. Under the old rules, he would be eligible for nursing home Medicaid 10 months later, or November 1,

2008. The new rules, however, work very differently. Let's say Uncle Harry is perfectly healthy when he makes his $70,000 gift on January 1, 2008. He then has a stroke four and a half years later, and enters the nursing home on June 1, 2012. Let's assume that he has only $1,500 in assets at that time, so he is otherwise eligible for Medicaid. The disqualification as a result of the $70,000 gift that he made four and a half years ago first starts to run when he applies for Medicaid on June 1, 2012. The disqualification period will run for 10 months from that time, and will end on March 31, 2013.

Who will pay for the nursing home during that time? Uncle Harry can't pay, because he is out of money. Unfortunately, no one knows who will pay. When Congress enacted the DRA, it left this very important question unanswered. Under the new rules, people such as Uncle Harry will be penalized for any gifts they have made during the past five years, regardless of the purpose of the gift. It does not matter that a moderate gift was made exclusively for a purpose other than to qualify for Medicaid. Therefore, the new law, for all practical purposes, makes gifting by people of moderate means very problematic.

Another drastic feature of the DRA concerns home equity. For a married couple, the home has always been a noncountable asset, and it remains so under the new law. With an unmarried person, the home has always been countable, with one exception. In New Hampshire, if an unmarried person owns a house, but had under $2,500 in other assets, he or she could still qualify for Medicaid on a temporary basis if the house were put on the market and sold within six months. If the house failed to sell within six months, extensions were routinely granted as long as the person was making active efforts to sell the house.

In Massachusetts, a home owned by an unmarried person is not countable, but the state will place a lien on it. In effect, then it is countable. The new law, however, contains an absolute bar on Medicaid eligibility for any unmarried person who has over $500,000 worth of equity in his or her home. Even if this person has no other assets at all, but has a house with over $500,000 in equity, he or she cannot obtain Medicaid, regardless of whether the house is on the market or not. Under the law, the states have the option to raise the $500,000 figure to $750,000. Massachusetts has done this, but New Hampshire has not.

Chapter 7
The Irrevocable
Medicaid Trust

*A*s we have demonstrated, the Deficit Reduction Act Medicaid rules are harsh and punitive. Any type of planning other than crisis planning must be done at least five years prior to a nursing-home stay, which means that pre-planning is more important than ever. Recall that under the old law, the transfer-of-asset penalty began to run when the transfer was made, and, for every month that has gone by, roughly another $7,000 worth of assets was protected. Under those rules, for every month that went by since the plan was done, you had another $7,000 under your belt. No matter what happened, you were ahead of game. Under the DRA, however, this has disappeared, since there is a flat, five-year waiting period. It is ironic that even though the intention of Congress was to slow down, if not stop, Medicaid planning, the DRA has made such planning more important now, and in more demand, than ever.

A key component of the Optimum Estate Plan must address the nursing home issue. While we endorse and encourage the purchase of long-term care insurance, we fully realize that most of our clients are, due to health issues, not insurable at any cost and many others simply cannot afford the cost. As elder law attorneys and estate planners, our clients look to us for legal ways to protect their assets and solve the issues that confront them now or may in the future. We see this as no different than rich clients who set up off-shore accounts, generation-skipping trusts, or creditor-protection trusts. Consequently, for most of our clients, the Irrevocable Medicaid Trust (also known as the "Medicaid" Trust) for nursing-home protection is a key document in their Optimum Estate Plan.

The Irrevocable Trust is similar in many ways to the Revocable Trust. The donor receives all of the income, but only the income from this trust, and, as trustee, the donor controls the investments held by the trust. Through the trust, the donor can buy and sell assets, including real estate, stocks, bonds, certificates of deposit, and the like. In fact, this type of trust can own, sell, and buy any type of investment other than a tax-deferred retirement account. Upon the donor's death, the trust assets will pass to the heirs without probate proceedings, and the trust will terminate. During the donor's lifetime, however, the trust is irrevocable and, due to the DRA, subject to a five-year look-back period.

Everyone uses the Medicaid Trust differently. Almost without exception, clients put their house and other real estate, such as a cottage on the lake, into the Medicaid Trust and leave their liquid assets in a Revocable Trust. Some people put their real estate and some portion of their liquid assets in the Medicaid Trust and the remainder in their financial assets in their Revocable Trust. The point is that the Revocable Trust/ Medicaid Trust combination must be tailored to each individual situation.

Even with a Medicaid Trust, you can still change your estate plan if you want to. For example: leaving money to grandchildren who were not even born when the trust was written. Or, say that one of your children is getting divorced, and you want to protect the inheritance from an ex-spouse. Or, one of your children has developed an alcohol or gambling problem. Or, one of your children dies before you, leaving children surviving. You can adjust your Medicaid Trust during these changing circumstances. The trust contains a feature known as a "Special Power of Appointment" (SPA). The SPA allows you to change your beneficiaries at death, when the trust is distributed. Say, for example, the beneficiaries of the trust are your three children: Dick, Jane, and Sally, and their children. At any time before your death, you can:

A. Adjust how much money Dick, Jane, and Sally are getting.
B. Disinherit Dick, Jane, or Sally.
C. Have the inheritance be held in trust for Dick, Jane, or Sally, instead of going to them out right or
D. Leave some or all of the money to the children of Dick, Jane, or Sally.

Thus, the Irrevocable Medicaid Trust can be adapted to changing circumstances.

Since most people use the Medicaid Trust to protect their real estate, though, let's take a look in more detail at how this works. You deed the house into the Medicaid Trust, and then need to wait five years for the protection to accrue. In other words, after five years, if you need care in a nursing home and apply for Medicaid, the house will not be counted. It will not have to be sold, and it can be passed on to your children. At any time before or after the five-year period, you are free to sell the house and buy another one if you want to, through the trust. If you do this, the new house will be protected without a new waiting period. If you choose to sell the house and not buy another one, then the money you received from the house becomes part of the trust will be protected. You will be able to receive the interest and dividends from this money, though the principal will remain in the trust until your death. If you put your house into an Irrevocable Medicaid Trust, you do not lose your capital gains advantages. That is, a single person can exempt the first $250,000 from capital gains, and a married couple can exempt the first $500,000, provided they otherwise qualify per the IRS rules. You do not lose these tax advantages if you put your house into the trust. The trust does not file a separate income tax return and the assets pass to your heirs with a "stepped up" tax basis at your death – the same as if the trust did not exist.

There are only two drawbacks of putting your house into the Medicaid Trust. First, you would not be able to obtain an equity loan or reverse mortgage. Second, it can become tricky if you have a property-tax exemption. In Massachusetts, if you have a property-tax exemption on your house, and you put it into the Medicaid Trust, you can maintain the exemption if the trust and/or deed contains a life estate. In New Hampshire, the law is the same. However, it is often not advisable to put a life estate in a New Hampshire Medicaid Trust, since doing so will allow the state to make a claim against a portion of the house proceeds after your death. Thus, if you have a tax exemption in New Hampshire, these issues need to be addressed carefully. In general, though, the Medicaid Trust is usually an ideal way to protect real estate.

Chapter 8
Putting Assets into Children's Names

A common Medicaid planning technique that you should generally never do is to put assets, such as house or certificates of deposit, in the names of your children. Even though many people are tempted to do this, it is very dangerous and should be avoided in almost all cases. There are three reasons why:

A. Liability

Any asset put into the names of your children is subject to their liabilities. So, if your house is in your daughter's name and she gets divorced, it can easily become part of her property settlement. Or, if your son - or his wife - gets very ill and needs nursing-home care, then your assets, which are in his name, will need to be spent on his care or his wife's care.

B. Loss of Control

If you put your assets into your children's names, you lose control over those assets. For example, say your house is in your son's name, and you want to sell it. You need to ask his permission, because, legally, it is his house. This is not a very good position to be in, because what if he can't give you the permission you need? Say, for example, he is being sued by his creditors and there is an attachment on the house. Maybe he does give you permission to sell, and you do so. Within a year, he files for bankruptcy. Your house, or the proceeds of sale, can be pulled into his bankruptcy case. Here is a tragic example that happens from time to time. Say your son marries a woman you simply can't stand. Your house is in your son's name, and he or she gets a serious illness and dies before you. He has a will leaving his assets (including your house!) to his wife. She is now your landlord. Obviously, you do not want to find yourself in this situation.

C. Tax Problems

Putting any appreciated asset, but especially your house, into your child's name can cause him or her to pay unnecessary capital gains taxes in two situations. First, say you want to sell the house. In most cases, you don't pay capital gains taxes when you sell your primary homestead. However, even if the house is in your child's name, it is your homestead, not his. Thus, if the house is sold, your child is not entitled to the capital gains exclusion, and any gain will be subject to capital gains taxes. Second, if you put your house in your child's name during life, then he not able to take advantage of the stepped-up tax basis at your death. You can avoid capital gains taxes if your child inherits your house at your death, instead of putting in the child's name while you're still alive. The

Medicaid Trust can be the ideal solution to avoid the problems caused by putting assets into your children's names.

Unfortunately, the DRA has left us with only three ways of doing nursing home pre-planning. First, you can put assets into your children's names. For the reasons we just went over, this is generally a big mistake. Second, you can buy long-term care insurance. For those people who can afford the insurance, and who qualify for it, this can be a good solution. However, most people can't afford it, and don't qualify for the insurance. Third, you use the Medicaid Trust. In our view, the Medicaid Trust is the most practical solution for most people, provided that it is done five years prior to a nursing-home stay.

Chapter 9
Crisis Medicaid Planning
For Married Couples

*P*rior to the DRA, there was a host of things that could be done for someone who was either in a nursing home or going into one shortly. Unfortunately, the DRA took away all but one of these techniques, but the one technique left is very powerful. It involves a type of financial instrument known as an "immediate annuity."

With an immediate annuity, you transfer a sum of money, usually to an insurance company, in exchange for monthly payments of principal and interest back to you. Think about a promissory note. In a promissory note transaction, you transfer a sum of money to a borrower. In exchange, the borrower pays you back in monthly installments of principal and interest. An immediate annuity is essentially the same thing. The difference between a promissory note and an immediate annuity, however, concerns the length of the payment term. With a promissory note, the payments can be for any length of time agreed to by lender and borrower. With an immediate annuity, the length of payments is based on the lender's life expectancy.

In the case of a married couple, an immediate annuity can shelter money, sometimes as much as 100 percent, from long-term care. This is the result of two different laws pertaining to spend-down in the case of a married couple. Recall from our discussion of the spend-down rules that the community spouse is permitted to keep half of the monetary assets, up to a cap of about $104,400. If a married couple has $200,000, the healthy spouse can keep $100,000, and the rest (except for $2,500) would have to be spent down. Significantly, the law says that the spend-down funds do not have to be spent on the nursing home! Those funds can be spent for any purpose, as long as fair value is received and as long as they are spent for the benefit of either spouse. The other relevant law concerns income. The income of the community spouse is completely exempt from the nursing home bills of the sick spouse. So, if one spouse is in the nursing home on Medicaid, and the other spouse has a job or otherwise gets income, then such income does not need to be used for the sick spouse's nursing home bill.

The key to annuity planning, then, is to re-structure the finances to convert assets that are fully countable for the nursing home to income for the healthy spouse, which is completely exempt. In the above example with a $100,000 spend-down, the healthy spouse uses the spend-down money to buy an immediate annuity, and the payments go to the healthy spouse. In this way, the sick one immediately qualifies for Medicaid, the monthly annuity payments go to healthy one, and all of the spend-down money has been preserved.

There are two drawbacks to the immediate annuity. First is the risk that the healthy spouse would need to go into a nursing home during the life of the annuity. In this event, the annuity payments will have to be spent on his or her care. Second is the risk that the healthy spouse dies before the annuity is all paid out. In this case, the remaining payments due need to go to the state, to the extent of Medicaid benefits paid for the sick spouse. In our view, the benefit of the immediate annuity greatly outweighs the risks in that the healthy spouse is completely protected. He or she can keep just about all of the assets, and, in many cases, still maintain some financial dignity.

Chapter 10
Federal and Massachusetts Estate Taxes

*W*hen someone dies, his or her estate may be subject to a tax known as the "estate tax." There are two levels of estate taxation: state and federal. Many people confuse estate taxes and inheritance taxes, but they are quite different. Inheritance taxes are levied on the beneficiary when he or she inherits assets. Estate taxes, by contrast, are levied not on the beneficiary, but rather on the assets a decedent owns at death. In other words, the tax is assessed and paid even before the beneficiary receives the inheritance. Generally, all of the assets that a decedent either owned or had a legal interest in at the time of death are subject to estate taxes, as are gifts over a certain amount that the decedent made during life. If the total of the assets owned at death and gifts are above a certain threshold, then the estate tax is imposed; if the assets are below that threshold, there is no tax. The executor has a choice of valuing the assets either at the date of death or at a so-called "alternate valuation date," that is, six months after death.

Certain deductions against the tax are allowed, including debts of the decedent, expenses of administering the estate, such as legal and accounting fees, charitable bequests, and assets passing either to the surviving spouse or to certain types of trusts for the benefit of the surviving spouse. If a tax is due, it must be paid within nine months from the date of death. A 2001 law known as the Economic Growth and Tax Relief Reconciliation Act states that the federal estate tax threshold will be $2 million for the years 2006 through 2008. The threshold will rise to $2.5 million in 2009. In 2010, there will be no federal estate tax at all, but in 2011, it will come back at a $1 million threshold.

In addition to the federal estate tax, individual states may have their own estate taxes. Before January 1, 2003, the estate taxes of many states, including Massachusetts, were tied to the federal estate tax. Under the laws in effect at that time, a percentage of the federal estate tax owed to the IRS would instead be paid to that state. The IRS, in turn, allowed estate taxes paid to the state to be a dollar-for-dollar credit against the federal tax. In this way, even though the state and federal estate tax loads were calculated separately, the tax paid to the state would be subtracted from the tax paid to the IRS. The states, in effect, were said to "sponge off" the federal tax, and hence these state estate taxes were known as "sponge taxes."

The Economic Growth and Tax Relief Reconciliation Act referred to above not only raised the thresholds that were subject to tax, but also phased out the availability of states to take advantage of, or "sponge off" the federal tax. Thus, the amount of money that states could raise from their own estate (sponge) taxes was lowered. That is, the increased exemption thresholds meant that fewer estates were subject to tax to begin with, and the sponge taxes imposed by those states were eliminated. To counter the expected decrease in revenue, some states, including Massachusetts, responded by "decoupling" their estate taxes from the federal estate tax. Decoupling means that the state estate tax would be calculated without reference to the federal estate tax. As of 2006, Illinois, Kansas, Maine, Maryland, Massachusetts, Minnesota, New Jersey, New York, North Carolina, Oregon, Rhode Island, Vermont, Virginia, Wisconsin, and District of Columbia have decoupled their estate taxes from the federal tax. In Massachusetts, decoupling became effective for the estates of people dying on or after January 1, 2003.

Under the Massachusetts version of decoupling, the filing thresholds and exemption amounts are lower for the state estate tax than for the federal estate tax. The Massachusetts filing threshold is $1 million. Therefore, at least until 2011, when the federal threshold also becomes $1 million, the filing requirements and exempt amounts must be determined separately for Massachusetts and federal estate tax purposes. Since the Massachusetts thresholds are lower than the federal thresholds, many more estates will be subject to the Massachusetts tax than the federal tax. Due to the run-up of real estate values in recent years, many people who do not think of themselves as wealthy will nevertheless be subject to the Massachusetts estate tax.

Prior to decoupling, when the Massachusetts tax was tied to the federal tax, a typical "dual revocable trust" estate plan would include an individual trust for each spouse. The trusts were each funded with approximately half of the total estate. After the death of the first spouse, his or her trust assets were allocated into two separate sub-trusts, the so-called "A-B Trust." The first sub-trust, funded with the amount exempt under federal law, is known as the "Family Trust."

Under the Family Trust, assets are available to the surviving spouse and children (but principally the surviving spouse) pursuant to an ascertainable standard, usually health, maintenance, education, and support. In this way, the trust assets can be used for the support of the surviving spouse, but are held in a way that those assets are not part of his or her taxable estate.

The rest of the assets belonging to the trust of the first spouse to die pass into another sub-trust called the "Marital Trust." The Marital Trust provides the surviving spouse with all of the income. It also often gives the trustee discretion to distribute principal as necessary for the surviving spouse's maintenance and health. Unlike the Family Trust, the Marital Trust is a part of the surviving spouse's taxable estate. In other words, when the second spouse dies, the Marital Trust assets are included among those subject to estate taxes. However, the Marital Trust is not taxed at the death of the first spouse, since it is subject to the 100 percent marital deduction. Upon the surviving spouse's death, the assets left in the Family Trust and Marital Trust pass to the heirs.

There are two different ways that the Family Trust and Marital Trust are funded. One way is called "formula funding." With formula funding, the executor does not have any discretion, since he or she is required, pursuant to a pre-determined formula, to allocate the assets between both trusts. The formula typically states that the trusts are funded in a way to make sure that there is no tax at the first death. The second way is known as "disclaimer funding." With disclaimer funding, the decision on how to fund the trusts is made by the surviving spouse. He or she "disclaims," or refuses to receive, assets of his or her choice. These disclaimed assets pass to the Family Trust. The assets not disclaimed go to the Marital Trust, or can go directly to the spouse.

Under the A-B type of estate plan, there are no estate taxes at the first death, and, at the second death, estate taxes are either eliminated or minimized. A simple example will show how this plan works. Say that Luke and Laura have an estate of $2.2 million, and Luke dies in 2011, when the federal estate tax exemption will be $1 million. They each have a simple will that leaves all of the assets to the surviving spouse, so when Luke dies in 2011, everything goes to Laura. An estate tax return will be filed, since Luke's estate is over the $1 million threshold. No tax will be due, though, since the money being left to Laura is subject to the Marital Deduction; i.e., it is deducted from the estate tax. Some years later, Laura dies, having an estate of $2.2 million. Since the estate tax exemption is only $1 million, a tax will be due on $1.2 million.

To avoid this result and minimize estate taxes, Luke and Laura enter into A-B Trusts. Each trust is funded with half the estate, or $1.1 million. Luke dies in 2011. The federal estate tax-exempt amount, or $1 million, goes to the Family Trust. The excess of $100,000 goes to the Marital Trust. The $100,000 that goes to the Marital Trust is subject to the 100 percent marital deduction, and the $1 million that goes to the Family Trust is not taxed either, as it is equal to the exempt amount. Laura has use of Luke's funds, as she is the beneficiary of both trusts. At Laura's death, she has $1.1 million in her name. The $1 million is not taxed, but the $100,000 in her name is taxed, as is the $100,000 in the Marital Trust that Luke left. Thus, the amount subject to tax at the second death is only $200,000.

Prior to decoupling in 2003, estate planning for a married couple with a taxable estate was not difficult, as the A-B Trust referred to above minimized, if not eliminated, all taxes. Now that the Massachusetts and Federal thresholds are different, though, the landscape has completely changed. If the Family Trust is funded with an amount of money that is less than the Federal exemption ($2 million) but more than the state exemption ($1 million) an estate tax will be due at the first death. For example, if $2 million were to go into the Family Trust, there would be a Massachusetts estate tax due on $1 million, and this tax would be $99,600.

Fortunately, the Massachusetts Department of Revenue (DOR) has addressed this issue. In a directive known as the "Technical Information Release 02 18," DOR has ruled that an executor may elect (i.e., claim) a marital deduction for Marital Trust property for Massachusetts' estate tax purposes without requiring the executor to make the same election for federal estate tax purposes. [3]   In other words, the Marital Trust for Massachusetts tax purposes can be different for the Martial Trust for federal estate tax purposes.   Therefore, the amount

---

3   Technically, this election is called a "QTIP Election." The term QTIP stands for Qualified Terminable Interest Property, which is derived from Section 2056(b)(7) of the Internal Revenue Code. Typically, and executor makes a QTIP election equal to the amount of the taxable estate over the federal exclusion amount. By definition, the federal exclusion amount is not subject to tax, and the property subject to the QTIP election is subject to the 100% marital deduction. Therefore, a proper QTIP election can eliminate estate tax at the first death.

going into the Family Trust is limited to the amount exempt for both state and federal purposes, i.e., $1 million. The difference between the Massachusetts exemption and the federal exemption goes to a special Massachusetts Marital Trust. The remainder of the estate goes to the Marital Trust allowed under federal law, or is distributed outright to the surviving spouse.

As a result of these changes, many Massachusetts estate plans need to be re-written, or, at the least re-evaluated. Essentially, instead of splitting the trust of the first to die into two trusts (the A and the B), the trust of the first to die might have to be split into three trusts, or three shares. First, there will be the Family Trust. Second, there will be the Massachusetts QTIP Marital Trust, and third there will be a federal Martial Trust, or a simple bequest to the surviving spouse. Any married couple with an estate over $1 million (or approaching $1 million) should be concerned about this issue.

Chapter 11
Trusts For Children with Special Needs

*P*lanning for this book on trusts for the average person and the Optimum Estate Plan would not be complete without some reference to trusts as a planning tool for children with "special needs." Frequently, the special need is a physical, mental, or developmental disability. Where these children are receiving governmental assistance, it is imperative that the parents plan their estates very carefully. If structured incorrectly, an inheritance otherwise designated for a particular beneficiary may disqualify that beneficiary from governmental assistance. In addition, almost every family is affected, or knows someone who is affected, by an adult child who has an addiction to alcohol, drugs, or gambling. While they are not receiving governmental benefits, their inheritance would be at risk were the child to receive it in a lump sum. Finally, many parents are concerned about children who do not have a disability or addiction, but who simply lack good judgment. Perhaps the adult child spends beyond his means and incurs substantial credit card debt, or is in a "bad" marriage and the parents are fearful that any inheritance to their child will be frittered away. These are real-life problems that impact countless families and require special attention and expertise. In all of these cases, the adult child (or minor child, as the case may be) has a "special need" which requires attention.

A. Special Needs Trusts for Children with Disabilities

Planning for children with disabilities is an area of concentration in our practice. This "niche" planning dovetails perfectly with our nursing-home planning for adult clients who, because of a stroke, memory loss, or other disability, may be facing a prolonged nursing-home stay. Any outright inheritance to a child with a disability is at risk to loss to the state, or may render the disabled child ineligible for state or federal assistance. This is simply not an acceptable result for folks who want to provide "extras" for their disabled child, to augment—but not replace—the governmental benefits their child is otherwise eligible to receive on account of his disability.

The bottom line is that to qualify for many governmental benefit programs, a disabled child may not, with certain exceptions, have assets in his own name exceeding $2,000. So, if a married couple with $300,000 in total assets leaves those assets equally among their three children, Sam, Sally, and Mike, each will receive $100,000; however, while Sam and Sally use their money to purchase boats or cars, pay down debt or take vacations, Mike sees his inheritance going to such things as clothing, medical, and housing expenses which, up until then, had been paid for by the government. In essence, this family's estate plan is flawed inasmuch as one child is effectively disinherited.

Throughout the years, we have seen folks try all sorts of self-help-type approaches to solving this dilemma. It is common for the family cited above to leave Mike's $100,000 to his brother, Sam with an unwritten promise by Sam to care for his brother. While this may seem to work, it can cause disastrous consequences, examples of which follow.

Say Sam dies before Mike and leaves his entire estate (including Mike's $100,000) to his wife, who remarries. Or maybe Sam's wife files for divorce and claims that Mike's $100,000 is part of the marital pool, subject to equal division. Perhaps Sam files for bankruptcy. Sam could be responsible in an automobile accident that causes personal injury to another and he is under-insured. Sam suffers a catastrophic injury or becomes confined to a nursing home. Sam has to fill out a student-aid form for his college-age child, only to realize that Mike's $100,000 is really Sam's asset for purposes of seeking financial assistance. There are many things that can go wrong, and it all could have been avoided through careful planning by the parents in their estate plan with the use of a "Special Needs" or "Supplemental Needs Trust" (SNT).

Special Needs Trusts come in a variety of forms. In the following examples, we will use a married couple, but Special Needs Trusts are equally as applicable to single folks who have a child with a disability.

1. There are stand-alone "living" or "inter vivos" Special Needs Trusts, which are separate and apart from the other trust(s) of the grantor.

2. There are Special Needs Trusts that are a part of the couple's other trust(s). In other words, the Special Needs Trust is incorporated as part

of the parents' trust and springs to life upon the death of both parents.

3. There are Special Needs Trusts that are set up under a will, which brings with it the supervision of Probate court and the disadvantages of the probate process discussed earlier.

4. There are Special Needs Trusts designed to supplement or augment what the government is providing in benefits (Supplemental Care SNT).

5. There are Special Needs Trusts that are designed to provide for the total, or nearly total, support of the child with a disability (General Support SNT).

6. There are Revocable Special Needs Trusts.

7. There are Irrevocable Special Needs Trusts.

A discussion of each type of trust could be extremely lengthy, but a brief overview is important.

The stand alone "living" or "inter vivos" SNT is designed to operate independently of the other parts of the parents' estate plan. It is a separate trust for the benefit of their disabled child. It often is funded by a life insurance policy on the parents' lives (usually a joint-and-survivor or second-to-die policy). In these cases, the insurance is the sole asset that goes into the trust. However, it may be augmented at the death of both parents by the share that is supposed to go to the special-needs child. A definite plus for this trust is that a grandparent or other relative may add or gift property to this trust at any time, during life or upon their deaths.

The more common SNT is one in which the parents simply incorporate it within their existing trust. Upon the second to die of both parents, the share intended for their disabled child does not go directly to him, but is held in further trust to be used as set forth by the particular and unique terms of the SNT. Since this type of SNT does not come into existence until the death of the parents, it may not be added to during the parents' lives by well-meaning grandparents, siblings, or other relatives.

The most common is the Supplemental Care SNT. This is artfully designed to augment, but not replace, the governmental benefits to which the beneficiary is otherwise entitled. Drafted correctly, this guarantees money for "extras" over and above what the modest (if not meager) governmental benefits provide.

A less common SNT is a General Support Trust. This is designed for those beneficiaries who have enough money in the trust (by life insurance or other assets) to provide the sole source of support. Because the cost of care is so expensive, these types of SNTs are used very sparingly.

There are Revocable Special Needs Trusts. In these, the parents reserve the right to change the trust at any time and take out any assets that are in it. The drawback is that the parents may wind up in a nursing home, subject to spend-down, and lose the assets in this trust. Additionally, creditors can attack this trust. It is far less certain that the assets in this trust will always be there for the disabled child.

There are Irrevocable Special Needs Trusts. In these instances, the parents give up ownership and control of the assets and cannot amend the trust if circumstances change. However, it is certain the assets in this trust will be there for the disabled child, even if the parents get sued or enter a nursing home or other such contingency.

There is no "one size fits all" Special Needs Trust and careful discussions with your attorney are needed to ensure the right one is in place for your child. A Special Needs Trust usually is quite extensive in granting the trustee discretion as to payments on behalf of a beneficiary. In the Supplemental Care SNT, it is common to provide the following as legitimate areas of expenditure:

1. Medical and dental expenses
2. Clothing
3. Housing
4. Transportation
5. Dietary needs
6. Purchase small gifts for relatives

This is not an exhaustive list by any means, but demonstrates some of the items to be covered in a well-drafted Special Needs Trust.

In addition, the trustee is often a sibling. Direction needs to be given in the trust itself and by the parents. Often, the following will be imposed on the trustee:

1. Requirement to visit beneficiary regularly.
2. Arrange for physical and dental examinations.
3. Evaluate education and training programs available to the beneficiary.
4. Determine appropriateness of residential opportunties available to the beneficiary.
5. Determine legal rights of beneficiary to public assitance.

The choice of trustee is crucial. Sometimes, a co-trustee arrangement is appropriate. In such as case, a bank or trust company acts as the financial trustee and a family member acts as the "personal" trustee. The personal trustee looks to the corporate trustee for funds to pay what the personal trustee deems necessary or desirable for the beneficiary.

B. Trusts for Children with Other Special Needs

Many is the instance when, through gambling addictions, drug additions, bad marriages, IRS problems, or simply bad management, parents establish "spendthrift" trusts for their children. These are designed to protect their children's inheritance, not from the state, but from the child himself (or a divorcing spouse or creditor). Spendthrift trusts are created as part of the parents' estate plan, incorporated within their trust, to limit what their child receives. These trusts can stretch the child's inheritance over time so a lump sum is not available for the child to consume or lose to divorce or other legal attachment. Such a trust can give the trustees (usually siblings) authority to distribute income and/or principal for the health, maintenance, support, and education of the child or a group consisting of the child and his children. Some trusts limit distribution of income only. Some allow for income, plus some percentage of principal each year to be payable to the child. Such a trust can even be flexible enough to permit the trustees to invest the child's share in an annuity, payable monthly to the child, over the child's life. This eliminates the child with the special need from pressuring his siblings, as trustees, to distribute more to him than is prudent. An Optimum Estate Plan must contain trusts to address these grave concerns shared by many, many families, rich and poor alike.

Chapter 12
Summary of Optimum Estate Planning Documents

*A*s we have seen, the Optimum Estate Plan contains four elements:

1. Revocable Trust:

This is the document that avoids probate. You have full control over the assets during life, and, at death, those assets pass to the heirs quickly and efficiently. This type of trust avoids probate only, and does not offer nursing home protection. For Massachusetts couples with over $1 million in assets, and United States couples with over $2 million in assets, two trusts would be necessary to avoid taxes.

2. Irrevocable Medicaid Trust:

This document avoids probate, and also protects the assets from long-term care. The trust is subject to a five-year look-back period. It is not generally used for all of the assets, but primarily for real estate and monetary assets that you know are to be passed down to the children.

3. Pour-over Will:

This is a simple will, that is meant to clean up any assets that are not in trust and do not have a designated beneficiary.

4. Durable Power of Attorney:

Used in the event of incapacity, it avoids guardianship proceedings. It can also be used by a healthy spouse to convert IRA/401k assets into immediate annuities, thereby protecting them from long-term care.

5. Advance Directives:

Also used in the event of incapacity, this document allows a designated person to make medical decisions, including the termination of life support if necessary. In New Hampshire, includes a Health Care Power of Attorney and living will declaration. In Massachusetts, includes a health care Proxy.

Let's look at a "real life" type case and see how the Optimum Estate Plan can help save time, money, and grief.

Stanley and Stella have been married for 45 years and are in their seventies. They have all of the documents that are part of the Optimum Estate Plan. Their assets are as follows:

House in Irrevocable Medicaid Trust	300,000
CDs, in Joint Revocable Trust	150,000
Stanley IRA, his name	100,000
Total	550,000

The analysis is the same whether they live in New Hampshire or Massachusetts. Stanley has a severe stroke and becomes incapacitated. He enters a nursing home. The state

Medicaid authorities do a resource assessment. The house is protected by the Medicaid Trust; Stella can keep can keep $104,400, and Stanley can keep $2,500. The balance of the assets needs to be spent down. Here is how Stella uses the Optimum Estate Planning documents.

First, since Stella is the health care agent for Stanley, she is allowed to make all of his medical decisions, and has authority to communicate with all of his medical providers. This makes her life much easier in that she did not have to go to probate court to seek guardianship.

Stella knows that she and Stanley can keep, between them, $106,900 ($104,400 + $2,500) and that she needs to spend down the sum of $143,100. Of this sum, $100,000 is in Stanley's IRA. Stella calls the IRA custodian and advises them of the situation. They ask her to send a copy of the Durable Power of Attorney, and she does so. Since she has Durable Power of Attorney, she is able to cash in Stanley's IRA and pay the taxes. She takes the remaining money after taxes, and combines it with enough money from the CDs to leave the protected $106,900. She puts the rest of the money into an immediate annuity, which pays her an income for the next five years. She applies for Medicaid assistance for Stanley, which is approved.

It is crucial that Stella had a Durable Power of Attorney. Without it, she would not have had any authority to talk to the IRA custodian, and would not have been able to purchase the annuity. She would have had to become Stanley's legal guardian, and then she would have been accountable to the Probate Court for the rest of Stanley's life. All of the money above $106,900 would have needed to be spent down. However, since she had power of attorney, she saved (after taxes) the money above $106,900 by putting it into the annuity. She will be able to keep this money, instead of having had to spend it. And, she was able to accomplish this privately, without hiring an attorney or go to Probate court. Because she has more money than she would have had without the annuity, she has greater peace of mind and better quality of life.

After being in the nursing home for a number of years, Stanley dies, and then a few years later, Stella becomes ill and enters a nursing home. Although she will have to use her remaining money to pay for her nursing-home care, the fact that she was able to pay privately assured her that she could get into the nursing home of her choice. However, recall that the house was in the Irrevocable Medicaid Trust. Therefore, the house is sheltered from nursing home costs, and Stella is able to receive Medicaid assistance. After she dies, the house, which has been protected by the irrevocable trust, is inherited by the children without going to probate.

The above example is one that we have seen played out many times over the years. As you can imagine, there are infinite variations on this theme. The point, though, is that the documents comprising the Optimum Estate Plan will save you and your family time, effort, and money, and will increase your security and peace of mind.

We will now focus on the proper planning techniques for your retirement accounts: how to minimize taxes and save them from disability.

Chapter 13
The Social Security Tax Trap

*I*n 1993, a modification to Social Security benefit taxation caused one of the largest tax increases to affect seniors in the history of our country. Very few seniors understood the significance of this change, and even fewer are taking advantage of planning techniques to reduce or eliminate this increase.

Before 1993, seniors paid taxes on half of their Social Security benefits if their combined income was $25,000 for individuals or $32,000 for married couples. In 1993, the portion of taxable Social Security increased to 85 percent, and individuals with "provisional" incomes above $34,000 and married couples with "provisional" incomes above $44,000 were subject to the higher rate of taxation. Those with provisional incomes below $25,000 and married couples with provisional incomes below $32,000 pay no taxes on their Social Security benefits.

Simply explained, provisional income is the sum of a person's wages if still employed, interest on his money, dividends from his investments, the net of capital gains/losses, any pension income (exclusive of Social Security), and any annuity or IRA distributions.

To this total, add one-half of the person's annual Social Security benefit, and if the sum of these is greater than $34,000 for a single taxpayer or $44,000 for a married couple, you fail the provisional income test, and your Social Security benefit is now taxed at the 85% threshold.

This increase has caused many seniors to pay much more in taxes over the last decade. Many have done nothing to counter the increase; they just pay more federal income tax.

Avoid the mistake. Review your most recent tax return. Specifically, review line 8a (interest). For many seniors this number is large because of the large stockpiles of cash in savings accounts, certificates of deposit, or treasuries. The interest this money produces in the bank or in government bonds may be causing you to "fail" the provisional income test. The interest being generated on these accounts may be the cause of the 85% Social Security threshold!

Consider a shift to tax-efficient or tax-deferred investments to reduce line 8a or 9b on the tax return to a level where you would "pass" the provisional income test and enjoy the Social Security benefit without counting it as a taxable event. This is what you expected when you entered the system in the first place.

There are several techniques to properly eliminate or reduce the implications of this tax problem.

Using a tax-deferred annuity to solve the problem is but one method. In addition to an annuity, shifting assets to "tax-efficient" planning also works well to reduce the exposure to the added tax.

Here is an example of a client couple that is currently "failing" the provisional income test:

Mr. and Mrs. John Client have been enjoying their retirement years. Their total household income is $55,000, and they have an adjusted gross income of $52,000. Not all Social Security benefits are taxable, as shown below.

Wages	$ 0
Interest (line 8a)	$ 20,000
Pension	$ 15,000
Social Security (line 20a)	$ 20,000

Determining how much of Social Security is taxable is a two-part process as described earlier.

First, determine the household income exclusive of Social Security benefits paid.

Interest (line 8a)	$ 20,000
Pension	$ 15,000
Household income	$ 35,000

Second, add the household income and one-half the annual Social Security benefit.

Household income	$ 35,000
One-half annual	
Social Security benefit	$ 10,000
	$ 45,000

$45,000 is greater than the top of the provisional income threshold of $44,000. As a result, this couple is taxed on 85 percent of their $20,000 Social Security benefit, increasing their taxable earnings by $6,850

How to Return Social Security Back to Tax-free Status. Mr. and Mrs. Client decide to shift most of their bank cash (which they don't plan to use but like to keep safe) into a fixed annuity. The interest is not taxable unless withdrawn. The results:

Wages	$ 0
Interest (line 8a)	$ 3,000 (1)
Pension	$ 15,000
Social Security	$ 20,000

First, determine the household income exclusive of Social Security benefits paid. Next, add one-half of the annual Social Security benefit.

Household income	$ 18,000
One-half Social Security benefit	$ 10,000
	$ 28,000

This $28,000 is less than the bottom provisional income test of $32,000. As a result, the clients are taxed on none of their Social Security benefit. This decreases their taxable earnings by nearly $7,000 accomplished simply by shifting the manner in which they allocate their savings. [4]

Many seniors make the mistake to focus on estate taxes and forget about using techniques that prevent the confiscation of wealth via the income tax. The income tax consequences of your actions or inactions can make a world of difference for you and your family. Spend some time reviewing your tax returns, and consider seeking advice to determine what planning opportunities would be best suited for your goals and objectives.

---

4   Client maintains over $50,000 in bank for emergencies
     or opportunities.

Chapter 14
The "Widow Tax Trap"

A major issue facing married seniors is the eventual "Widow Tax Trap" that will occur when a spouse dies, leaving the surviving spouse as a "single" tax filer. Married people enjoy much higher thresholds of marginal Federal income tax brackets than those who are single. See the 2008 tables below:

Married couples filing a joint return in 2008:

- 10% on the income between $0 and $16,050
- 15% on the income between $16,050 and $65,100
- 25% on the income between $65,100 and $131,450
- 28% on the income between $131,450 and $200,300
- 33% on the income between $200,300 and $357,700
- 35% on the income over $357,700

Single people filing an individual return in 2008:

- 10% on income between $0 and $8,025
- 15% on the income between $8,025 and $32,550
- 25% on the income between $32,550 and $78,850
- 28% on the income between $78,850 and $164,550
- 33% on the income between $164,550 and $357,700
- 35% on the income over $357,700

Most retired couples are within the 15% federal income tax bracket where up to $65,100 is taxed in the 15% marginal rate. When a spouse passes away, the survivor will begin filing as a single tax payer the year after the spouse's death. Marginal income thresholds for single people in the 10% and 15% bracket are one-half of what they were when they were filing as a married couple! This change in thresholds often causes a major tax increase for the surviving spouse who oftentimes will now find herself suddenly "jumping brackets" from the 10% into the 15% bracket, or from the 15% bracket into the 25% bracket, because many retirees plan their pensions to provide 100% survivorship income. This option was selected to provide security for the surviving spouse. Unfortunately, because of the Social Security Tax Trap (outlined earlier), many survivors will now pay taxes on 85% of the reduced Social Security benefit because she is failing the provisional income test. We say "reduced" because the widow/widower is not allowed to continue enjoying both her and her husband's full Social Security benefits after his passing. In addition, the "stockpile" of IRA accounts that have been amassed over a lifetime of saving will usually be "rolled over" to the surviving spouse. The widow owning the entire IRA account must take Required Minimum Distributions (after age 70 ½) and these distributions will further complicate tax planning issues. These circumstances are played out time and time again for those who do not plan in advance to minimize this problem.

The combination of the Social Security Tax Trap, the "Widow" Tax trap, and untaxed IRA accounts may wreak havoc in survivorship planning. We will spend the next few chapters working through how to build a proper "estate" plan for your IRA to avoid these traps.

Chapter 15
The "Stretch" IRA

*T*he single largest asset for many retirees other than their primary residence is their Individual Retirement Account ("IRA"), and most are completely unaware of the tax nightmare that awaits the beneficiaries of these accounts if the account holders have not properly established a plan to pass this tax-deferred asset to their spouses and children.

In 2001, the Internal Revenue Service overhauled the rules pertaining to mandatory distributions from IRA accounts, and as a result, some excellent planning opportunities are now available. Today, with proper planning, your IRA accounts can live on for your family long after you are gone.

After an IRA owner's death, a spouse can roll the IRA into his/her name. This "spousal" rollover approach is widely known as a preferred planning technique to protect the spouse. Where most IRA planning goes awry is when the spouse dies and the children plan to inherit the asset. If the surviving spouse names a "designated" beneficiary of the IRA account, the beneficiary can withdraw the funds from the IRA over his or her life expectancy after the parent dies. The planning potential of this technique is tremendous. Under the old rules, the beneficiary would simply cash out the parent's IRA account and pay the income taxes on the distribution, resulting in massive taxes for most beneficiaries. With the new rules, the beneficiaries have a planning opportunity to take simply the RMD (Required Minimum Distribution) based on their life expectancy, and the remaining account balance can continue to grow on a tax-deferred basis. This technique is known as the "Stretch IRA." The beneficiary can elect to remove more than the required distribution at any time if he needs additional funds.

Case Study

Mr. John Smith, age 65, has an IRA valued at $250,000. Let's assume that he earns 6% on this IRA and will be taking only his Required Minimum Distributions once he is age 70½. Assume he has one child whom he names beneficiary of his IRA. His child, Bill, is age 40. Mr. Smith's required distribution schedule will look like this:

Mr. John Smith's IRA
Assuming 6% return on investment and taking only RMDs

Year	Age	Required Distribution	Account Value 12/31
2008	65	$0	$265,000
2009	66	$0	$280,900
2010	67	$0	$297,754
2011	68	$0	$315,619
2012	69	$0	$334,556
2013	70	$12,210	$342,420
2014	71	$12,922	$350,043

2015	72	$13,674	$357,372
2016	73	$14,469	$364,346
2017	74	$15,309	$370,898
2018	75	$16,196	$376,956
2019	76	$17,134	$382,439
2020	77	$18,040	$387,346
2021	78	$19,081	$391,505
2022	79	$20,077	$394,918
2023	80	$21,119	$397,495
2024	81	$22,206	$399,138
2025	82	$23,341	$399,745
2026	83	$24,524	$399,205
2027	84	$25,755	$397,403
2028	85	$26,852	$394,395
2029	86	$27,971	$390,088
2030	87	$29,111	$384,382

Now let's assume Mr. Smith lives until age 87. When he dies, his son is age 63. His son has two choices:

First, he can simply cash out Dad's IRA (no stretch) and pay the income taxes due.

Lump Sum Account Liquidation in 2031

Total distributions	$384,382
Federal income tax on total distribution	<u>$121,309</u>
Net after tax to Bill	$263,073

35% top tax bracket.

Second, Bill stretches the IRA.

Required Distributions from 2031 through 2053

Total distributions	$841,738
Federal income taxes	$215,122
Net after-tax income	$626,616

25% median tax bracket.

With no stretch planning, Bill will inherit $263,073, but with the stretch IRA planning, he will inherit $626,616. With proper planning, the IRA account will become a family heirloom and a multigenerational asset transferring event. (The above calculation assumes Bill is married filing a joint return and has taxable income of $50,000, excluding the required distributions.)

How the Stretch Technique Works

Bill must begin taking required distributions from his father's IRA based on his own life expectancy starting the year following his father's death. His father's IRA is now worth $390,512 and his son, now age 63, must take a minimum distribution of $16,933.

Mr. Bill Smith's Inherited IRA
Assuming 6% return on investment and taking only RMDs

Year	Age	Required Distribution	Account Value 12/31
2031	63	$16,933	$390,512
2032	64	$17,996	$395,946
2033	65	$19,128	$400,575
2034	66	$20,334	$404,276
2035	67	$21,619	$406,914
2036	68	$22,989	$408,339
2037	69	$24,451	$408,388
2038	70	$26,012	$406,879

2039	71	$27,679	$403,613
2040	72	$29,461	$398,369
2041	73	$31,368	$390,904
2042	74	$33,411	$380,947
2043	75	$35,603	$368,201
2044	76	$37,959	$352,335
2045	77	$40,498	$332,977
2046	78	$43,244	$309,711
2047	79	$46,226	$282,068
2048	80	$49,486	$249,507
2049	81	$53,087	$211,391
2050	82	$57,133	$166,942
2051	83	$61,830	$115,128
2052	84	$67,722	$54,313
2053	85	$57,572	$0

Bill must be listed as a "designated" beneficiary on the IRA beneficiary election form for the stretch option to be valid. The easiest way to understand a "designated beneficiary" is a beneficiary with a birth date. When the son notifies the custodian of the death of his father, he will most likely need to furnish a certified death certificate and also establish a beneficiary IRA account with the custodian. At that time, the IRA provider will move the assets from the decedent's IRA into the "inherited" IRA account. Keep in mind the account will stay in the name of the deceased for the beneficiary's benefit but does not roll over into the son's IRA accounts.

Potential Pitfalls

If Mr. Smith failed to name a beneficiary or he named his estate as the beneficiary, his son would have only up to five years from the date of death to remove the value from the IRA account. This does not leave much planning opportunity.

If Mr. Smith names a trust as beneficiary, there are numerous potential negative consequences for his son. In most cases, it is best to name the beneficiaries of the IRA accounts by name. The son will either use the five-year rule to remove the IRA assets or, best case, he may be able to use the remaining life expectancy of Mr. Smith. Obviously Mr. Smith's life expectancy would be much shorter than his son's.

The current custodian who holds the IRA may not honor the stretch technique. This is a common but little understood problem with the IRA account. You should review the custodial agreement signed when you established your IRA account to see if the provider will allow the stretch. Surprisingly, not all custodians allow this to occur. The income tax ramifications of not stretching are severe. If your custodian does not honor the stretch, you may want to consider moving your IRA account to a provider who does.

The power of the "Stretch IRA" provides you with the opportunity to focus on multigenerational planning while maintaining 100% control of the account during your life.

Chapter 16
The "Stretch" Roth IRA

*A*s we have just learned, "Stretch IRA" planning can be very powerful in estate planning. An even better technique is the "Stretch" Roth IRA. "The Jobs and Growth Tax Relief Reconciliation Act of 2003" has created wonderful planning opportunities for the informed senior. The tax code was enacted back in 1913, and with the tax package of 2003, we are enjoying the "luxury" of some of the lowest tax brackets in our country's history.

A quick review of current tax brackets (2008):

<u>10%</u> Married couples earning less than $16,050 and single people earning less than $8,025 in taxable earnings are taxed in the 10% tax bracket.

<u>15%</u> Married couples who earn less than $65,100 and single people who earn less than $32,550 in taxable earnings are taxed in the 15% tax bracket.

<u>25%</u> Married couples who earn less than $131,450 and single people who earn less than $78,850 in taxable earnings are taxed in the 25% bracket.

Food for thought: Our government is allocating a huge

amount of resources to fight the war on terrorism and the war in Iraq. Medicare is in a state of crisis. Social Security is heading towards insolvency. The Pension Benefit Guarantee Corporation (PBGC) is having solvency issues, and our nation's deficit and debt are reaching epic proportions while at the same time we are enjoying some of the lowest tax brackets since the tax code was adopted! Sooner or later, our nation will have to change either its spending or our tax structure.

Retirees have been trained to avoid taking distributions from their IRA portfolios for two primary reasons. First, many are comfortably living on their Social Security benefits and pension incomes. Second, when retirees take money out of the retirement account, they must do something they have been trained to avoid... pay income tax on the distribution. Many seniors delay the distribution event until it becomes mandatory at age 70½. (See IRS publication 590.)

This is often a major financial planning mistake! One of the largest planning mistakes retirees make when it comes to the IRA account is waiting too long to begin the distribution process. Here's why. The IRA account is tax-deferred, not tax-free. When one spouse dies, the survivor is now forced to file a tax return as a "single taxpayer." Review the brackets for single people versus married couples. Married couples enjoy much wider 10% and 15% tax brackets versus single people. In fact, the brackets are cut in half! Many widows and widowers suddenly find themselves jumping into higher brackets and pay more income taxes when they become single taxpayers: the "Widow Tax" trap. Unfortunately, this is not a rare occurrence; it happens all too often. Finally, upon the survivor's death, the IRA is often taxed to the heirs at even higher tax brackets!

With some foresight, you can make the outcome much different.

First, review your tax return. Many seniors actually enjoy the 0% tax bracket, and most married couples are within the 10% or 15% tax bracket. The technique described next works best within these tax brackets. Taxes are eventually due on the IRA. The question is: should you pre-pay the tax now at the low brackets or delay?

Step 1: If you are already over 70½, take the MRD as required by law out of your IRA. If under age 70½, proceed directly to step 2.

Step 2: Using your previous year's tax return as a guide, run the math to determine what sources of income were reported and what the taxable income was. This is to be a guide. Please remember to consider any additional withdrawals you have taken from your IRA accounts, capital gains from the sale of any investments you hold, pension increases, and/or wages if you worked any part of the year.

Step 3: With this information, forecast what the taxable income will be for the current year.

Step 4: If you are "enjoying the luxury" of the 0%, 10% or 15% bracket, consider "converting" IRA assets to the Roth IRA to the extent that you will remain within these low brackets. Caveat: you must review your Social Security benefits for inclusion into this calculation.

When you properly utilize this technique, you will create a tax-free legacy. There will be no required distributions or additional taxes for the surviving spouse. When one spouse dies, a jump in brackets is less likely because there is no required distribution to pass through the single person's federal tax bracket. Roth IRA distributions do not affect Social Security provisional income. Even if there is not sufficient time to convert the entire IRA to the Roth, you have still reduced the IRA account value for the MRD calculation, resulting in a positive impact on your overall tax planning.

The Roth IRA provides a "one-two" punch by allowing you to reduce the pitfalls in the tax code for single taxpayers while creating a tax-free legacy for the family. Here is how it works:

Mr. John Smith, age 65, has a ROTH IRA valued at $250,000. Let's assume that he earns 6% on this IRA and plans to leave the account alone because he is not required to take distributions. Assume he has one child whom he names beneficiary of his ROTH IRA. His child (Bill) is age 40. Mr. Smith's portfolio will grow over his lifetime as follows:

Mr. John Smith's ROTH IRA
Assuming 6% Return on Investment and NO distributions

Year	Age	Required Distribution	Account Value 12/31
2008	65	0	$265,000
2009	66	0	$280,900
2010	67	0	$297,754
2011	68	0	$315,619
2012	69	0	$334,556
2013	70	0	$354,630
2014	71	0	$375,908
2015	72	0	$398,462
2016	73	0	$422,370

2017	74	0	$447,712
2018	75	0	$474,575
2019	76	0	$503,049
2020	77	0	$533,232
2021	78	0	$565,226
2022	79	0	$599,140
2023	80	0	$635,088
2024	81	0	$673,193
2025	82	0	$713,585
2026	83	0	$756,400
2027	84	0	$801,784
2028	85	0	$849,891
2029	86	0	$900,884
2030	87	0	$954,937

Now let's assume Mr. Smith lives until age 87. When he dies, his son is age 63. His son has two choices

First, he can simply cash out Dad's IRA (no stretch).

Lump Sum Account Liquidation in 2031

Total distributions	$970,166
Federal income tax on total distribution	$ 0
Net after-tax to Bill	$970,166

NO TAX because account was a ROTH IRA. Account is much larger than traditional stretch IRA because there were no required minimum distributions to withdraw from the ROTH.

Second, Bill stretches the ROTH IRA.

Required Distributions from 2031 through 2053

Total distributions	$2,091,170
Federal income taxes	$ 0
Net after-tax income	$2,091,170

With no stretch planning, Bill will inherit a sizeable tax free account of $954,937, much better than the $626,616 after-tax benefit he would have accomplished with the traditional Stretch IRA discussed in the previous chapter. The stretch ROTH produces a stellar $2,091,170. This was all accomplished by executing proper planning when the IRA was valued at $250,000! With proper planning, the ROTH IRA account will create a tax-free legacy for you, your spouse, and your family.

How the Stretch ROTH Technique Works

Unlike his father John, who is NOT required to take distributions from the ROTH IRA, Bill must begin taking required distributions from his father's ROTH IRA based on his own life expectancy starting the year following his father's death. His father's ROTH IRA is now worth $954,937 and Bill, now age 63, must take a minimum distribution of $42,068 TAX FREE.

Mr. Bill Smith's Inherited ROTH IRA
Assuming 6% Return on Investment and Taking Only RMDs

Year	Age	Required Distribution	Account Value 12/31
2031	63	$42,068	$970,166
2032	64	$44,708	$983,668

2033	65	$47,520	$995,168
2034	66	$50,516	$1,004,362
2035	67	$53,709	$1,010,914
2036	68	$57,114	$1,014,455
2037	69	$60,746	$1,014,577
2038	70	$64,623	$1,010,829
2039	71	$68,764	$1,002,714
2040	72	$73,191	$989,686
2041	73	$77,928	$971,140
2042	74	$83,003	$946,405
2043	75	$88,449	$914,740
2044	76	$94,303	$875,321
2045	77	$100,612	$827,229
2046	78	$107,432	$769,430
2047	79	$114,840	$700,756
2048	80	$122,940	$619,861
2049	81	$131,885	$525,168
2050	82	$141,937	$414,741
2051	83	$153,608	$286,017
2052	84	$168,246	$134,933
2053	85	$143,029	$0

The ROTH IRA is amongst the most powerful financial and estate planning techniques available today. This technique has been around since 1998, yet very few people understand the value and take advantage of the opportunity.

Chapter 17
Net Unrealized Appreciation

*M*any retirees have accumulated very large 401(k) balances or other qualified plans as a result of a career's worth of savings. For some, a large percentage of your plan consists of highly appreciated individual company stock. The tax savings you can generate using the NUA (net unrealized appreciation) technique can make a significant impact on your financial and estate planning.

Unfortunately, many retirees and many advisors make a fundamental mistake: they roll the qualified plan rich in employer stock to an IRA. Often retirees and advisors assume rolling to an IRA is the only option available. On the surface, this seems like the standard operating procedure, but if this option is exercised, you may cost your family thousands of dollars in additional taxes they should not have to pay!

A. NUA Explained

NUA occurs when an employer-sponsored plan allows the employee to purchase employer securities as part of the qualified retirement plan. The Internal Revenue Service treats these securities held inside the plan differently than it treats other assets, such as cash and mutual funds when an employee retires. When the employee rolls over his qualified plan to an IRA, he has the opportunity to withdraw his employer securities and pay income tax on the cost basis (not the current value) and capital gains tax on the gain if he sells the employer securities. The cash, mutual funds, or other investment accounts will roll over to the IRA and are not taxed until withdrawn. (See IRS publication 575.)

Case Study

Mr. Smith, age 65, has a 401(k) plan valued at $500,000. $250,000 is mutual funds and $250,000 is company stock. The basis on the company stock is $50,000. Assume Mr. Smith is in the 25% federal income tax bracket.

Option 1: Normal roll-over approach

Mr. Smith rolls the entire account to an IRA. Any normal distributions he takes will be taxed in the 25% federal income tax bracket. At age 70½, he will be forced to take required minimum distributions (RMD) and pay taxes on these distributions in his then applicable (assumed 25%) tax bracket. (See IRS Publication 590.)

Option 2: NUA rollover approach

Mr. Smith rolls the stock out of the 401(k) plan. The basis on the stock is $50,000, and he must pay ordinary income tax on the basis of $12,500 ($50,000 x 25% tax rate). The stock is transferred to a non-qualified account. No additional taxes are owed on the stock until Mr. Smith sells it. Assume he does sell the stock. He pays capital gain tax on the sale vs.

ordinary income and is thus taxed at 15% (current maximum capital gain tax rate), not 25%. This creates an immediate tax savings of 10%. Shares sold under this technique are taxed at long-term capital gain tax rates (up to the NUA) regardless of the length of time between the roll-out and the sale of the stock and short- or long-term gains on any additional gain beyond the NUA based on the time of sale. If he does not sell the stock, there are no additional taxes beyond the ordinary income tax due on the roll-out. All other remaining funds are rolled to an IRA.

B. Benefits of NUA

First, by utilizing the NUA approach, you will reduce your overall tax burden on the 401(k) plan and have the opportunity to use capital gain tax rates vs. ordinary income tax on $200,000 of the value of the account.

Second, by reducing the amount rolling into the IRA, you will reduce the required distribution amounts when you reach age 70½. Required minimum distributions are calculated on the year-end balance of the IRA, and if you remove the value of the stock from the account, it will not be included in the RMD calculation.

Third, capital gain tax rates are significantly lower than the current income tax rates.

These tax savings can be used to fund long-term care and other estate preservation strategies using funds that otherwise would have been lost to taxes!

C. Drawbacks

This technique is designed primarily for those above

age 59½. The early distribution penalties apply to those who elect this option under age 59½, and a 10% early distribution penalty will apply. The technique, however, may still be a viable option under these circumstances, as the penalty tax only pertains to the "basis" of the roll-out and not the full value of the stock.

NUA does not enjoy a "stepped-up basis" at death. When reviewing your overall estate planning objectives, you must be aware that, unlike other highly appreciated securities you may own, the NUA stock will not receive the increase to market value at death and may present a large capital gain tax to the beneficiary. A plan to liquidate out of the NUA stock may be necessary to prevent erosion due to the tax the beneficiary will pay.

Chapter 18
What To Do From Here?

*I*f the readers of this book are like most of our clients, they are senior citizens who have worked a lifetime building up a nest egg. They have worked hard, paid their mortgage, paid their taxes, provided for their families, and have put money in the bank. Rather than complain or give up when life put obstacles in their path, they have kept on doing what they were taught as children: be diligent in their work and make the best of it.

This generation has been the most successful in history in saving and investing money, and, as this book has shown, there are two forces that can strip them of what they have saved over a lifetime and make it much harder to pass anything to their children and grandchildren: the nursing home and the tax system. Dying in our country is less expensive than becoming disabled along the way. This is a sad but true fact. Most folks have taken time to create an estate plan for death but they have yet to properly plan for what may happen with assets should they live. This is called a "Life Plan." If you have made it to the end of this book, congratulations! Your next course of action should be to create your "Life Plan; the Optimum Estate Plan."